# UK The classics Air Fryer Cookbook 2024

*2600 Days Air Fryer Recipes is a comprehensive guide that will enhance your cooking experience.*

**Shelley A. Snell**

# CONTENTS

## Fish And Seafood Recipes ....................................................................... 57

## Recipe Index ................................................................. **91**

# Introduction

The Air Fryer, a kitchen appliance that has taken the culinary world by storm, has revolutionized the way we cook. This remarkable device has gained immense popularity due to its ability to prepare delicious and healthier meals with a fraction of the oil traditionally used in frying. In this comprehensive guide, we will delve into the advantages of using an Air Fryer, share some essential tips and tricks for maximizing its potential, and provide guidance on how to clean and maintain this innovative appliance.

## Advantages of Air Fryers

### Healthier Cooking

One of the most significant advantages of using an Air Fryer is its ability to cook food with little to no oil. Instead of submerging ingredients in a deep fryer filled with oil, the Air Fryer uses hot air circulation to achieve that crispy, golden-brown texture. This method significantly reduces the calorie and fat content of your favorite fried foods, making them a healthier option.

### Versatility

Air Fryers are incredibly versatile and can handle a wide range of cooking tasks. Besides frying, they can also bake, roast, grill, and even reheat leftovers. This versatility allows you to prepare a variety of dishes, from crispy fries and chicken wings to roasted vegetables and baked goods, all in one appliance.

### Time Efficiency

Air Fryers are designed to cook food quickly and evenly. The rapid hot air circulation ensures that your meals are ready in a fraction of the time it would take in a conventional oven or stovetop. This time efficiency makes Air Fryers a convenient choice for busy individuals and families.

### Easy to Use

Using an Air Fryer is simple and user-friendly. Most models come with digital controls and pre-set cooking programs for popular dishes, making it easy for even beginners to achieve delicious results. Just set the temperature and cooking time, and the Air Fryer does the rest.

### Energy Efficiency

Compared to traditional ovens, Air Fryers are energy-efficient. They require less electricity to operate, making them an eco-friendly choice while helping you save on your energy bills.

## Air Fryer Usage Tips and Techniques

### Preheat the Air Fryer

Just like with conventional ovens, it's essential to preheat your Air Fryer. Preheating ensures that the hot air is evenly distributed from the beginning, resulting in better-cooked food. Follow the manufacturer's instructions for preheating times and temperatures.

### Use the Right Amount of Oil

While Air Fryers use significantly less oil than deep frying, using a small amount of oil or cooking spray can enhance the flavor and texture of your dishes. Experiment with different types of oils and seasonings to achieve the desired taste.

### Don't Overcrowd the Basket

To ensure even cooking and that coveted crispy texture, avoid overcrowding the Air Fryer basket. Leave some space between the food items to allow hot air to circulate freely. If you have a large batch to cook, consider doing it in multiple rounds.

### Shake or Flip Food

During the cooking process, periodically shake or flip the food in the basket. This helps to ensure that all sides are evenly cooked and prevents sticking.

### Adjust Temperatures and Times

Every Air Fryer model is different, so it's essential to experiment and adjust cooking temperatures and times to suit your preferences. Start with the recommended settings and make adjustments as needed.

# Cleaning and Maintenance

Proper cleaning and maintenance are crucial to keep your Air Fryer in optimal condition.

### Unplug and Cool Down

Always unplug your Air Fryer and allow it to cool down before cleaning. This prevents any accidents and ensures your safety.

### Remove and Wash Components

Most Air Fryers have removable components like the basket, tray, and pan. Take them out and wash them with warm, soapy water. Some models are dishwasher-safe, but it's best to check the manufacturer's instructions.

### Wipe the Interior

Use a damp cloth or sponge to wipe the interior of the Air Fryer. Be gentle and avoid using abrasive materials that could damage the non-stick coating.

### Clean the Heating Element

If your Air Fryer has a visible heating element, use a soft brush or cloth to clean it. Make sure it's completely dry before reassembling the appliance.

### Regular Maintenance

Perform regular maintenance by checking for any signs of wear and tear. If you notice any issues with the heating element, fan, or other components, contact the manufacturer or a qualified technician for repairs.

# Bread And Breakfast
## Bacon Muffins

Servings: 8
Cooking Time: 15 Minutes
**Ingredients:**

- 6 large eggs
- 3 slices of cooked and chopped bacon
- ½ cup of chopped green and red bell pepper
- ½ cup of shredded cheddar cheese
- ¼ cup of shredded mozzarella cheese
- ¼ cup of chopped fresh spinach
- ¼ cup of chopped onions
- 2 tablespoons milk
- Black pepper and salt, to taste

**Directions:**

1. Put eggs, milk, black pepper, and salt into a suitable mixing bowl.
2. Whisk it until well combined.
3. Add in chopped bell peppers, spinach, black peppers, onions, ½ of shredded cheeses, and crumbled bacon. Mix it well.
4. First, place the silicone cups in the air fryer, then pour the egg mixture into them and add the remaining cheeses.
5. At 300 degrees F/ 150 degrees C, preheat your Air fryer.
6. Cook the prepared egg muffins for almost 12–15 minutes.
7. Serve warm and enjoy your Egg Muffins with Bacon!

## Coconut Muffins With Jalapeno

Servings: 8
Cooking Time: 15 Minutes
**Ingredients:**

- 5 eggs
- ⅓ cup coconut oil, melted
- 2 teaspoons baking powder
- 3 tablespoons erythritol
- 3 tablespoons jalapenos, sliced
- ¼ cup unsweetened coconut milk
- 2/3 cup coconut flour
- ¾ teaspoon salt

**Directions:**

1. At 325 degrees F/ 160 degrees C, preheat your air fryer.
2. In a suitable bowl, mix together coconut flour, baking powder, erythritol, and salt.
3. Add eggs, jalapenos, coconut milk, and coconut oil until well combined.
4. Pour batter into the silicone muffin molds and place into the air fryer basket.
5. Cook muffins for almost 15 minutes.
6. Serve and enjoy.

# Avocado Quesadillas

Servings:4
Cooking Time: 11 Minutes
**Ingredients:**

- 4 eggs
- 2 tablespoons skim milk
- Salt and ground black pepper, to taste
- Cooking spray
- 4 flour tortillas
- 4 tablespoons salsa
- 2 ounces (57 g) Cheddar cheese, grated
- ½ small avocado, peeled and thinly sliced

**Directions:**

1. Preheat the air fryer to 270ºF (132ºC).
2. Beat together the eggs, milk, salt, and pepper.
3. Spray a baking pan lightly with cooking spray and add egg mixture.
4. Bake for 8 minutes, stirring every 1 to 2 minutes, until eggs are scrambled to the liking. Remove and set aside.
5. Spray one side of each tortilla with cooking spray. Flip over.
6. Divide eggs, salsa, cheese, and avocado among the tortillas, covering only half of each tortilla.
7. Fold each tortilla in half and press down lightly. Increase the temperature of the air fryer to 390ºF (199ºC).
8. Put 2 tortillas in air fryer basket and air fry for 3 minutes or until cheese melts and outside feels slightly crispy. Repeat with remaining two tortillas.
9. Cut each cooked tortilla into halves. Serve warm.

# Cheddar Broccoli Quiche

Servings: 2
Cooking Time: 10 Minutes
**Ingredients:**

- 8 small broccoli florets
- 2 eggs
- ½ cup of heavy cream
- 2 tablespoons of cheddar, grated
- Black pepper and salt, to taste

**Directions:**

1. At 325 degrees F/ 160 degrees C, preheat your air fryer.
2. Grease 2 5-inch ceramic dishes with oil or cooking spray.
3. Put eggs, salt, heavy cream, and black pepper into a suitable mixing bowl.
4. Whisk it well then put broccoli florets on the dish's bottom and pour the egg mixture over them.
5. Cook it at 325 degrees F/ 160 degrees C for almost 10 minutes.
6. Serve warm.

# Grilled Butter Sandwich

Servings: 1
Cooking Time: 10 Minutes
**Ingredients:**

- 2 slices of bread
- 3 slices of any cheese
- 1 tablespoon of melted butter

**Directions:**

1. At 350 degrees F/ 175 degrees C, preheat your air fryer.
2. Spread the melted butter over 1 side of each piece of bread.
3. Arrange the cheese slices over the bread and make a sandwich.
4. Put it in the air fryer and fry at 350 degrees F/ 175 degrees C for almost 10 minutes almost.
5. Serve warm and enjoy your Grilled Butter Sandwich!
6. Sandwich Fillings: Spread some pesto inside the sandwich and use just mozzarella cheese.
7. Put cooked bacon and use only cheddar cheese.
8. Add some fresh spinach with Swiss cheese inside the sandwich.

# Frittata

Servings: 2 Servings
Cooking Time: 30 Minutes
**Ingredients:**

- 4 eggs
- ½ cup of cooked and chopped sausage
- ½ cup of shredded cheddar cheese
- 1 chopped green onion
- 2 tablespoons of chopped red bell pepper
- 1 pinch of cayenne powder

**Directions:**

1. Preheat your air fryer to 350°F. Lightly grease a 6-inch cake pan with some oil.
2. Whisk eggs in a large bowl. Add the sausage, bell pepper, cheese, onion, and cayenne powder, and mix until well combined.
3. Transfer the egg mixture into the prepared cake pan and cook in the air fryer at 350°F for 18–20 minutes. Check the readiness using a toothpick; it should come out clean after inserting in the center.
4. Serve with any fresh vegetables and greens. Enjoy your Frittata!

# Spinach Bacon Spread

Servings: 4
Cooking Time: 10 Minutes
**Ingredients:**
- 2 tablespoons coconut cream
- 3 cups spinach leaves
- 2 tablespoons cilantro
- 2 tablespoons bacon, cooked and crumbled
- Salt and black pepper to the taste

**Directions:**
1. Combine coconut cream, spinach leaves, salt, and black pepper in a suitable baking pan.
2. Transfer the baking pan into your air fryer and cook at 360 degrees F/ 180 degrees C for 10 minutes.
3. When cooked, transfer to a blender and pulse well.
4. To serve, sprinkle the bacon on the top of the mixture.

# Mozzarella Rolls

Servings: 6
Cooking Time: 6 Minutes
**Ingredients:**
- 6 wonton wrappers
- 1 tablespoon keto tomato sauce
- ½ cup Mozzarella, shredded
- 1 ounce pepperoni, chopped
- 1 egg, beaten
- Cooking spray

**Directions:**
1. Before cooking, heat your air fryer to 400 degrees F/ 205 degrees C.
2. Spritz the cooking spray over an air fryer basket with cooking spray.
3. Mix the pepperoni, shredded Mozzarella cheese, and tomato sauce in a big bowl until homogenous.
4. Separate the mixture onto wonton wraps.
5. Roll the wraps into sticks.
6. Use the beaten eggs to brush the sticks.
7. Arrange evenly on the air fryer basket and cook in your air fryer for 6 minutes and flip the sticks halfway through cooking.

# Sausage And Egg Breakfast Burrito

Servings: 6

Cooking Time: 30 Minutes

**Ingredients:**

- 6 eggs
- Salt
- Pepper
- Cooking oil
- ½ cup chopped red bell pepper
- ½ cup chopped green bell pepper
- 8 ounces ground chicken sausage
- ½ cup salsa
- 6 medium (8-inch) flour tortillas
- ½ cup shredded Cheddar cheese


**Directions:**

1. In a medium bowl, whisk the eggs. Add salt and pepper to taste.

2. Place a skillet on medium-high heat. Spray with cooking oil. Add the eggs. Scramble for 2 to 3 minutes, until the eggs are fluffy. Remove the eggs from the skillet and set aside.

3. If needed, spray the skillet with more oil. Add the chopped red and green bell peppers. Cook for 2 to 3 minutes, until the peppers are soft.

4. Add the ground sausage to the skillet. Break the sausage into smaller pieces using a spatula or spoon. Cook for 3 to 4 minutes, until the sausage is brown.

5. Add the salsa and scrambled eggs. Stir to combine. Remove the skillet from heat.

6. Spoon the mixture evenly onto the tortillas.

7. To form the burritos, fold the sides of each tortilla in toward the middle and then roll up from the bottom. You can secure each burrito with a toothpick. Or you can moisten the outside edge of the tortilla with a small amount of water. I prefer to use a cooking brush, but you can also dab with your fingers.

8. Spray the burritos with cooking oil and place them in the air fryer. Do not stack. Cook the burritos in batches if they do not all fit in the basket. Cook for 8 minutes.

9. Open the air fryer and flip the burritos. Cook for an additional 2 minutes or until crisp.

10. If necessary, repeat steps 8 and 9 for the remaining burritos.

11. Sprinkle the Cheddar cheese over the burritos. Cool before serving.

# Simple Cherry Tarts

Servings: 6
Cooking Time: 10 Minutes
**Ingredients:**

- For the tarts:
- 2 refrigerated piecrusts
- ⅓ cup cherry preserves
- 1 teaspoon cornstarch
- Cooking oil
- For the frosting:
- ½ cup vanilla yogurt
- 1 ounce cream cheese
- 1 teaspoon stevia
- Rainbow sprinkles


**Directions:**

1. Place the piecrusts on a flat surface. Make use of a knife or pizza cutter, cut each piecrust into 3 rectangles, for 6 in total. I discard the unused dough left from slicing the edges.
2. In a suitable bowl, combine the preserves and cornstarch. Mix well.
3. Scoop 1 tablespoon of the preserve mixture onto the top ½ of each piece of piecrust.
4. Fold the bottom of each piece up to close the tart.
5. Press along the edges of each tart to seal using the back of a fork.
6. Sprinkle the breakfast tarts with cooking oil and place them in the air fryer.
7. Cook for almost 10 minutes
8. Allow the breakfast tarts to cool fully before removing from the air fryer.
9. To make the frosting:
10. In a suitable bowl, mix the yogurt, cream cheese, and stevia. Mix well.
11. Spread the breakfast tarts with frosting and top with sprinkles, and serve.

# Tasty English Breakfast

Servings: 8
Cooking Time: 20 Minutes
**Ingredients:**

- 8 sausages
- 8 bacon slices
- 4 eggs
- 1 16-ounce can have baked beans
- 8 slices of toast

**Directions:**

1. Spread the sausages and bacon slices in your air fryer and air fry for almost 10 minutes at a 320 degrees F/ 160 degrees C.
2. Add the baked beans to a ramekin, then place another ramekin and add the eggs and whisk.
3. Increase the temperature to 290 degrees F/ 145 degrees C.
4. Place it in your air fryer and cook it for 10 minutes more.
5. Serve and enjoy!

# Hard-boiled Eggs

Servings: 2
Cooking Time: 16 Minutes
**Ingredients:**

- 4 eggs
- ¼ teaspoon salt

**Directions:**

1. Cook the eggs in your air fryer at 250 degrees F/ 120 degrees C for 16 minutes.
2. When the cooking time is up, cool the eggs in ice water.
3. Then peel the eggs and cut them into halve.
4. Season the egg halves with salt and serve.

# Flavorful Scrambled Eggs With Chorizo

Servings: 2
Cooking Time: 13 Minutes
**Ingredients:**

- 1 dash of Spanish paprika
- 1 dash of oregano
- 3 large eggs, beaten
- 1 tablespoon olive oil
- ½ zucchini, sliced
- ½ chorizo sausage, sliced

**Directions:**

1.   Prepare all the recipe ingredients.
2.   At 350 degrees F/ 175 degrees C, preheat your air fryer. Fry the zucchini in olive oil, season with salt and cook for 2-3 minutes.
3.   Add chorizo to the zucchini and cook for another 5-6 minutes.
4.   Fill with the egg mixture and send it back to the air fryer for 5 minutes, take out the basket and stir for every minute until tender.
5.   Serve and Enjoy.

# Veggie Frittata

Servings: 4
Cooking Time:8 To 12 Minutes
**Ingredients:**

- ½ cup chopped red bell pepper
- ⅓ cup minced onion
- ⅓ cup grated carrot
- 1 teaspoon olive oil
- 6 egg whites
- 1 egg
- ⅓ cup 2 percent milk
- 1 tablespoon grated Parmesan cheese

**Directions:**

1.   In a 6-by-2-inch pan, stir together the red bell pepper, onion, carrot, and olive oil. Put the pan into the air fryer. Cook for 4 to 6 minutes, shaking the basket once, until the vegetables are tender.
2.   Meanwhile, in a medium bowl, beat the egg whites, egg, and milk until combined.
3.   Pour the egg mixture over the vegetables in the pan. Sprinkle with the Parmesan cheese. Return the pan to the air fryer.
4.   Bake for 4 to 6 minutes more, or until the frittata is puffy and set.
5.   Cut into 4 wedges and serve.

# Banana Churros With Oatmeal

Servings:2

Cooking Time: 15 Minutes

**Ingredients:**

- For the Churros:
- 1 large yellow banana, peeled, cut in half lengthwise, then cut in half widthwise
- 2 tablespoons whole-wheat pastry flour
- ⅛ teaspoon sea salt
- 2 teaspoons oil (sunflower or melted coconut)
- 1 teaspoon water
- Cooking spray
- 1 tablespoon coconut sugar
- ½ teaspoon cinnamon
- For the Oatmeal:
- ¾ cup rolled oats
- 1½ cups water

**Directions:**

1. To make the churros
2. Put the 4 banana pieces in a medium-size bowl and add the flour and salt. Stir gently. Add the oil and water. Stir gently until evenly mixed. You may need to press some coating onto the banana pieces.
3. Spray the air fryer basket with the oil spray. Put the banana pieces in the air fryer basket and air fry for 5 minutes. Remove, gently turn over, and air fry for another 5 minutes or until browned.
4. In a medium bowl, add the coconut sugar and cinnamon and stir to combine. When the banana pieces are nicely browned, spray with the oil and place in the cinnamon-sugar bowl. Toss gently with a spatula to coat the banana pieces with the mixture.
5. To make the oatmeal
6. While the bananas are cooking, make the oatmeal. In a medium pot, bring the oats and water to a boil, then reduce to low heat. Simmer, stirring often, until all the water is absorbed, about 5 minutes. Put the oatmeal into two bowls.
7. Top the oatmeal with the coated banana pieces and serve immediately.

# Olives And Eggs Medley

Servings: 4
Cooking Time: 20 Minutes
**Ingredients:**

- 2 cups black olives, pitted and chopped
- 4 eggs, whisked
- ¼ teaspoon sweet paprika
- 1 tablespoon cilantro, chopped
- ½ cup cheddar, shredded
- A pinch of salt and black pepper
- Cooking spray

**Directions:**

1. Add the olives into the beaten egg in a bowl and mix together all the ingredients except the cooking spray.
2. At 350 degrees F/ 175 degrees C, heat your air fryer in advance.
3. Grease your baking pan with the cooking spray.
4. Pour the olive-egg mixture evenly in the pan.
5. Transfer the pan inside your air fryer and cook for 20 minutes.
6. Serve the medley on plates. Enjoy your breakfast.

# Grilled Cheese Sandwich

Servings: 1 Sandwich
Cooking Time: 15 Minutes
**Ingredients:**

- 2 slices of sandwich bread
- 3 slices of any cheese you like (mozzarella, cheddar, etc.)
- 1 tablespoon of melted butter

**Directions:**

1. Preheat your air fryer to 350ºF.
2. Spread the melted butter over one side of each piece of bread. Put the cheese slices on the bread and make a sandwich.
3. Put it in the air fryer and fry at 350ºF for 10 minutes.
4. Serve warm and enjoy your Grilled Cheese Sandwich!

# Baked Potato Breakfast Boats

Servings:4

Cooking Time: 20 Minutes

**Ingredients:**

- 2 large russet potatoes, scrubbed
- Olive oil
- Salt
- Freshly ground black pepper
- 4 eggs
- 2 tablespoons chopped, cooked bacon
- 1 cup shredded cheddar cheese

**Directions:**

1. Poke holes in the potatoes with a fork and microwave on full power for 5 minutes.
2. Turn potatoes over and cook an additional 3 to 5 minutes, or until the potatoes are fork tender.
3. Cut the potatoes in half lengthwise and use a spoon to scoop out the inside of the potato. Be careful to leave a layer of potato so that it makes a sturdy "boat."
4. Lightly spray the fryer basket with olive oil. Spray the skin side of the potatoes with oil and sprinkle with salt and pepper to taste.
5. Place the potato skins in the fryer basket skin side down. Crack one egg into each potato skin.
6. Sprinkle ½ tablespoon of bacon pieces and ¼ cup of shredded cheese on top of each egg. Sprinkle with salt and pepper to taste.
7. Air fry until the yolk is slightly runny, 5 to 6 minutes, or until the yolk is fully cooked, 7 to 10 minutes.


# Simple Scotch Eggs

Servings:4

Cooking Time: 25 Minutes

**Ingredients:**

- 4 large hard boiled eggs
- 1 (12-ounce / 340-g) package pork sausage
- 8 slices thick-cut bacon
- Special Equipment:
- 4 wooden toothpicks, soaked in water for at least 30 minutes

**Directions:**

1. Slice the sausage into four parts and place each part into a large circle.
2. Put an egg into each circle and wrap it in the sausage. Put in the refrigerator for 1 hour.
3. Preheat the air fryer to 450°F (235°C).
4. Make a cross with two pieces of thick-cut bacon. Put a wrapped egg in the center, fold the bacon over top of the egg, and secure with a toothpick.
5. Air fry in the preheated air fryer for 25 minutes.
6. Serve immediately.

# Strawberry And Peach Toast

Servings: 4
Cooking Time: 2 Minutes
**Ingredients:**

- 2-4 slices bread
- Strawberries, as needed
- 1 peach, corned and sliced
- 1 teaspoon sugar
- Cooking spray
- ¼ cup cream cheese
- 1 teaspoon cinnamon

**Directions:**

1. Prepare all the recipe ingredients from the list.
2. Spray both sides of the bread with olive oil. Place in the preheated air fryer basket and Cook at almost 375 degrees F/ 190 degrees C for 1 minute on each side.
3. Slice strawberries and peaches and prepare the rest of the ingredients.
4. Spread toast thickly of cream cheese, garnish with strawberries and peach, sprinkle with almonds and cinnamon mixture if you like.
5. Serve with smoothies, coffee or tea.

# Parmesan Ranch Risotto

Servings:2
Cooking Time: 30 Minutes
**Ingredients:**

- 1 tablespoon olive oil
- 1 clove garlic, minced
- 1 tablespoon unsalted butter
- 1 onion, diced
- ¾ cup Arborio rice
- 2 cups chicken stock, boiling
- ½ cup Parmesan cheese, grated

**Directions:**

1. Preheat the air fryer to 390ºF (199ºC).
2. Grease a round baking tin with olive oil and stir in the garlic, butter, and onion.
3. Transfer the tin to the air fryer and bake for 4 minutes. Add the rice and bake for 4 more minutes.
4. Turn the air fryer to 320ºF (160ºC) and pour in the chicken stock. Cover and bake for 22 minutes.
5. Scatter with cheese and serve.

# Appetizers And Snacks
## Pickles With Egg Wash

Servings:4

Cooking Time: 8 Minutes

**Ingredients:**

- 2 pickles, sliced
- 1 tablespoon dried dill
- 1 egg, beaten
- 2 tablespoons flax meal

**Directions:**

1. Coat the sliced pickles with the egg, then sprinkle with the dried ill and flax meal.
2. Arrange the pickles to the basket of your air fryer and cook for 8 minutes at 400 degrees F/ 205 degrees C.

## Squash Chips With Sauce

Servings: 4

Cooking Time: 25 Minutes

**Ingredients:**

- ½ cup seasoned breadcrumbs
- ½ cup Parmesan cheese, grated
- Sea salt, to taste
- Ground black pepper, to taste
- ¼-teaspoon oregano
- 2 yellow squash, cut into slices
- ½ tablespoon grapeseed oil
- Sauce:
- ½ cup Greek-style yogurt
- 1 tablespoon fresh cilantro, chopped
- 1 garlic clove, minced
- Freshly ground black pepper, to your liking

**Directions:**

1. Thoroughly combine the seasoned breadcrumbs, Parmesan, salt, black pepper, and oregano in a prepared shallow bowl.
2. Dip the yellow squash slices in the prepared batter and press to make it adhere.
3. Place the squash slices in the basket of your air fryer and brush them with grapeseed oil.
4. Cook at 400 degrees F/ 205 degrees C for 12 minutes. Shake the basket periodically to ensure even cooking. Work in batches.
5. Meanwhile, whisk the sauce ingredients; place in your refrigerator until ready to serve.
6. Enjoy!

# Zucchini And Potato Tots

Servings:4
Cooking Time: 20 Minutes
**Ingredients:**

- 1 large zucchini, grated
- 1 medium baked potato, skin removed and mashed
- ¼ cup shredded Cheddar cheese
- 1 large egg, beaten
- ½ teaspoon kosher salt
- Cooking spray

**Directions:**

1. Preheat the air fryer to 390ºF (199ºC).
2. Wrap the grated zucchini in a paper towel and squeeze out any excess liquid, then combine the zucchini, baked potato, shredded Cheddar cheese, egg, and kosher salt in a large bowl.
3. Spray a baking pan with cooking spray, then place individual tablespoons of the zucchini mixture in the pan and air fry for 10 minutes. Repeat this process with the remaining mixture.
4. Remove the tots and allow to cool on a wire rack for 5 minutes before serving.

# Parmesan Steak Nuggets

Servings: 4
Cooking Time: 18 Minutes
**Ingredients:**

- 1 pound beef steak, cut into chunks
- 1 large egg, lightly beaten
- ½ cup pork rind, crushed
- ½ cup parmesan cheese, grated
- ½ teaspoon salt

**Directions:**

1. Add egg in a suitable bowl.
2. In a suitable bowl, mix pork rind, cheese, and salt.
3. Dip each steak chunk in egg then coat with pork rind mixture and place on a plate.
4. Place in refrigerator for 30 minutes.
5. Grease its air fryer basket with cooking spray.
6. At 400 degrees F/ 205 degrees C, preheat your air fryer.
7. Place steak nuggets in air fryer basket and cook for almost 15-18 minutes or until cooked.
8. Serve and enjoy.

# Cauliflower Bites

Servings: 4
Cooking Time: 15 Minutes
**Ingredients:**

- 1 tbsp. Italian seasoning
- 1 cup flour
- 1 cup milk
- 1 egg, beaten
- 1 head cauliflower, cut into florets

**Directions:**

1. After mixing the flour, milk, egg, and Italian seasoning well, coat the cauliflower with the mixture and drain the excess liquid.
2. Spray the florets with cooking spray and cook them in your air fryer at 390 degrees F/ 200 degrees C for 7 minutes.
3. After that, shake and cook for 5 minutes more.
4. Cool down before serving.

# Roasted Almonds With Paprika

Servings: 8
Cooking Time: 8 Minutes
**Ingredients:**

- 2 cups almonds
- ¼ teaspoon black pepper
- 1 teaspoon paprika
- 1 tablespoon garlic powder
- 1 tablespoon soy sauce

**Directions:**

1. Add black pepper, paprika, garlic powder, and soy sauce in a suitable bowl and stir well.
2. Add almonds and stir to coat.
3. Grease its air fryer basket with cooking spray.
4. Add almonds in air fryer basket and cook for 6-8 minutes at 320 degrees F/ 160 degrees C.
5. Serve and enjoy.

# Cinnamon Apple Chips

Servings:4
Cooking Time: 10 Minutes
**Ingredients:**

- Olive oil
- 2 apples, any variety, cored, cut in half, and cut into thin slices
- 2 heaped teaspoons ground cinnamon

**Directions:**

1. Spray a fryer basket lightly with oil.
2. In a medium bowl, toss the apple slices with the cinnamon until evenly coated.
3. Place the apple slices in the fryer basket in a single layer. You may need to cook them in batches.
4. Air fry for 4 to 5 minutes. Shake the basket and cook until crispy, another 4 to 5 minutes.

# Spinach Dip With Bread Knots

Servings:6
Cooking Time: 16 To 21 Minutes
**Ingredients:**

- Nonstick cooking spray
- 1 (8-ounce) package cream cheese, cut into cubes
- ¼ cup sour cream
- ½ cup frozen chopped spinach, thawed and drained
- ½ cup grated Swiss cheese
- 2 green onions, chopped
- ½ (11-ounce) can refrigerated breadstick dough
- 2 tablespoons melted butter
- 3 tablespoons grated Parmesan cheese

**Directions:**

1. Spray a 6-by-6-by-2-inch pan with nonstick cooking spray.
2. In a medium bowl, combine the cream cheese, sour cream, spinach, Swiss cheese, and green onions, and mix well. Spread into the prepared pan and bake for 8 minutes or until hot.
3. While the dip is baking, unroll six of the breadsticks and cut them in half crosswise to make 12 pieces.
4. Gently stretch each piece of dough and tie into a loose knot; tuck in the ends.
5. When the dip is hot, remove from the air fryer and carefully place each bread knot on top of the dip, covering the surface of the dip. Brush each knot with melted butter and sprinkle Parmesan cheese on top.
6. Bake for 8 to 13 minutes or until the bread knots are golden brown and cooked through.

# Lemony Endive In Curried Yogurt

Servings:6
Cooking Time: 10 Minutes
**Ingredients:**

- 6 heads endive
- ½ cup plain and fat-free yogurt
- 3 tablespoons lemon juice
- 1 teaspoon garlic powder
- ½ teaspoon curry powder
- Salt and ground black pepper, to taste

**Directions:**

1. Wash the endives, and slice them in half lengthwise.
2. In a bowl, mix together the yogurt, lemon juice, garlic powder, curry powder, salt and pepper.
3. Brush the endive halves with the marinade, coating them completely. Allow to sit for at least 30 minutes or up to 24 hours.
4. Preheat the air fryer to 320ºF (160ºC).
5. Put the endives in the air fryer basket and air fry for 10 minutes.
6. Serve hot.

# Fried Bacon Slices

Servings: 11
Cooking Time: 10 Minutes
**Ingredients:**

- 11 bacon slices

**Directions:**

1. Place ½ bacon slices in air fryer basket.
2. Cook at almost 400 degrees F/ 205 degrees C for almost 10 minutes.
3. Cook remaining ½ bacon slices using same steps.
4. Serve and enjoy.

# Poutine With Waffle Fries

Servings:4
Cooking Time: 15 To 17 Minutes
**Ingredients:**

- 2 cups frozen waffle cut fries
- 2 teaspoons olive oil
- 1 red bell pepper, chopped
- 2 green onions, sliced
- 1 cup shredded Swiss cheese
- ½ cup bottled chicken gravy

**Directions:**

1. Preheat the air fryer to 380ºF (193ºC).
2. Toss the waffle fries with the olive oil and place in the air fryer basket. Air fry for 10 to 12 minutes, or until the fries are crisp and light golden brown, shaking the basket halfway through the cooking time.
3. Transfer the fries to a baking pan and top with the pepper, green onions, and cheese. Air fry for 3 minutes, or until the vegetables are crisp and tender.
4. Remove the pan from the air fryer and drizzle the gravy over the fries. Air fry for 2 minutes, or until the gravy is hot.
5. Serve immediately.

# Southwest Stuffed Mushrooms

Servings: 4
Cooking Time:8 To 12 Minutes
**Ingredients:**

- 16 medium button mushrooms, rinsed and patted dry
- ⅓ cup low-sodium salsa
- 3 garlic cloves, minced
- 1 medium onion, finely chopped
- 1 jalapeño pepper, minced (see Tip)
- ⅛ teaspoon cayenne pepper
- 3 tablespoons shredded pepper Jack cheese
- 2 teaspoons olive oil

**Directions:**

1. Remove the stems from the mushrooms and finely chop them, reserving the whole caps.
2. In a medium bowl, mix the salsa, garlic, onion, jalapeño, cayenne, and pepper Jack cheese. Stir in the chopped mushroom stems.
3. Stuff this mixture into the mushroom caps, mounding the filling. Drizzle the olive oil on the mushrooms. Air-fry the mushrooms in the air fryer basket for 8 to 12 minutes, or until the filling is hot and the mushrooms are tender. Serve immediately.

# Panko Crusted Chicken Tenders

Servings: 4
Cooking Time: 10 Minutes
**Ingredients:**

- 12 ounces chicken breasts, cut into tenders
- 1 egg white
- ⅛ cup flour
- ½ cup panko bread crumbs
- Black pepper and salt, to taste

**Directions:**

1. At 350 degrees F/ 175 degrees C, preheat your air fryer. and grease its air fryer basket.
2. Season the chicken tenders with some black pepper and salt.
3. Coat the chicken tenders with flour, then dip in egg whites and then dredge in the panko bread crumbs.
4. Arrange the prepared tender in the air fryer basket and cook for about 10 minutes.
5. Dish out in a platter and serve warm.

# Vidalia Onion Blossom

Servings: 4
Cooking Time: 25 Minutes
**Ingredients:**

- 1 large Vidalia onion
- 1½ cups all-purpose flour
- 1 teaspoon garlic powder
- 1 teaspoon paprika
- Salt
- Pepper
- 2 eggs
- 1 cup milk
- Cooking oil

**Directions:**

1. Cut off the pointy stem end of the onion. Leave the root end intact. Peel the onion and place it cut-side down. The root end of the onion should be facing up.
2. Starting about ½ inch from the root end, cut downward to make 4 evenly spaced cuts. In each section, make 3 additional cuts. There should be 16 cuts in the onion.
3. Turn the onion over and fluff out the "petals."
4. Place the flour in a large bowl and season it with the garlic powder, paprika, and salt and pepper to taste.
5. In another large bowl, whisk the eggs. Add the milk and stir. This will form a batter.
6. Place the onion in the bowl with the flour mixture. Use a large spoon to cover the onion petals in flour.
7. Transfer the onion to the batter. Use a spoon or basting brush to cover the onion completely.
8. Return the onion to the flour mixture. Cover completely.
9. Wrap the battered onion in foil and place in the freezer for 45 minutes.
10. Spray the air fryer basket with cooking oil. Unwrap the foil covering and place the onion in the air fryer basket. Cook for 10 minutes.
11. Open the air fryer. Spray the onion with cooking oil. If areas of the onion are still white from the flour, focus the spray on these areas.
12. Cook for an additional 10 to 15 minutes, or until crisp.

# Mexican Beef Muffins With Tomato Sauce

Servings:4
Cooking Time: 15 Minutes
**Ingredients:**

- 1 cup ground beef
- 1 teaspoon taco seasonings
- 2 oz. Mexican blend cheese, shredded
- 1 teaspoon tomato sauce
- Cooking spray

**Directions:**

1. Thoroughly mix up ground beef and taco seasonings in a mixing bowl.
2. Spray the muffin molds with cooking spray.
3. Transfer the ground beef mixture in the muffin molds. Place the cheese and tomato sauce on the top.
4. Transfer the muffin molds in the prepared air fryer and cook them for 15 minutes at 375 degrees F/ 190 degrees C.
5. When cooked, serve and enjoy.

# Garlic Cauliflower Appetizer

Servings: 2
Cooking Time: 20 Minutes
**Ingredients:**

- 5 cups cauliflower florets
- ½ teaspoon Kosher salt
- ½ teaspoon paprika
- ½ teaspoon garlic powder
- 2 tablespoons avocado oil

**Directions:**

1. Prepare a large bowl, add the Kosher salt, avocado oil, paprika, garlic powder, and cauliflower florets. Coat well.
2. Arrange the coated cauliflower to the basket of your air fryer and cook at 390 degrees F/ 200 degrees C for 18 minutes, shaking the basket halfway through.
3. Cooking in batches is suggested.
4. When done, serve immediately. Bon appétit!

# Delicious Zucchini Crackers

Servings:12

Cooking Time: 20 Minutes

**Ingredients:**

- 1 cup zucchini, grated
- 2 tablespoons flax meal
- 1 teaspoon salt
- 3 tablespoons almond flour
- ¼ teaspoon baking powder
- ¼ teaspoon chili flakes
- 1 tablespoon xanthan gum
- 1 tablespoon butter, softened
- 1 egg, beaten
- Cooking spray

**Directions:**

1. Squeeze the zucchini to remove the vegetable juice and transfer to a large bowl.
2. Thoroughly mix up the flax meal, salt, almond flour, baking powder, chili flakes and xanthan gum.
3. Add butter and egg. Knead the non- sticky dough.
4. Place the mixture on the baking paper and cover with another baking paper.
5. Roll up the dough into the flat square.
6. After this, remove the baking paper from the dough surface.
7. Cut it on medium size crackers.
8. Prepare the air fryer basket by lining it with baking paper, and then put the crackers inside it.
9. Spray them with cooking spray. Cook them for 20 minutes at 355 degrees F/ 180 degrees C.
10. Serve and enjoy.

# Crispy Mozzarella Sticks

Servings:8
Cooking Time: 6 To 7 Minutes

**Ingredients:**

- 1 egg
- 1 tablespoon water
- 8 eggroll wraps
- 8 Mozzarella string cheese "sticks"

**Directions:**

1. Preheat the air fryer to 390ºF (199ºC).
2. Beat together egg and water in a small bowl.
3. Lay out eggroll wraps and moisten edges with egg wash.
4. Place one piece of string cheese on each wrap near one end.
5. Fold in sides of eggroll wrap over ends of cheese, and then roll up.
6. Brush outside of wrap with egg wash and press gently to seal well.
7. Place in air fryer basket in a single layer and air fry for 5 minutes. Air fry for an additional 1 or 2 minutes, if necessary, or until they are golden brown and crispy.
8. Serve immediately.

# Potatoes With Bacon

Servings: 4
Cooking Time: 30 Minutes

**Ingredients:**

- 4 potatoes, scrubbed, halved, cut lengthwise
- 1 tbsp. olive oil
- Salt and black pepper to taste
- 4 oz. bacon, chopped

**Directions:**

1. Brush the potatoes with olive oil and season with salt and pepper.
2. Transfer the seasoned potatoes to the cooking basket and arrange it to your air fryer.
3. Cook them at 390 degrees F/ 200 degrees C for 30 minutes, flipping and topping with bacon halfway through the cooking time.
4. When done, serve and enjoy.

# Chicken Bites With Coconut

Servings: 4
Cooking Time: 20 Minutes
**Ingredients:**

- 2 teaspoons garlic powder
- 2 eggs
- Salt and black pepper to the taste
- ¾ cup coconut flakes
- Cooking spray
- 1 pound chicken breasts, skinless, boneless, and cubed

**Directions:**

1. In a bowl, put the coconut in and mix the eggs with garlic powder, salt and pepper in a second one.
2. Dredge the chicken cubes in eggs and then in coconut.
3. Arrange all the prepared chicken cubes to the basket.
4. Grease with cooking spray and cook them at 370 degrees F/ 185 degrees C for 20 minutes.
5. When cooked, place the chicken bites on a platter and serve as an appetizer.

# Pigs In A Blanket

Servings:6
Cooking Time: 14 Minutes
**Ingredients:**

- 24 cocktail smoked sausages
- 6 slices deli-sliced Cheddar cheese, each cut into 8 rectangular pieces
- 1 (8-ounce / 227-g) tube refrigerated crescent roll dough

**Directions:**

1. Preheat the air fryer to 350ºF (177ºC).
2. Unroll the crescent roll dough into one large sheet. If your crescent roll dough has perforated seams, pinch or roll all the perforated seams together. Cut the large sheet of dough into 4 rectangles. Then cut each rectangle into 6 pieces by making one slice lengthwise in the middle and 2 slices horizontally. You should have 24 pieces of dough.
3. Make a deep slit lengthwise down the center of the cocktail sausage. Stuff two pieces of cheese into the slit in the sausage. Roll one piece of crescent dough around the stuffed cocktail sausage, leaving the ends of the sausage exposed. Pinch the seam together. Repeat with the remaining sausages.
4. Air fry in 2 batches for 7 minutes, placing the sausages seam-side down in the basket. Serve hot.

# Poultry Recipes

## Yellow Curry Chicken Thighs With Peanuts

Servings:6

Cooking Time: 20 Minutes

**Ingredients:**

- ½ cup unsweetened full-fat coconut milk
- 2 tablespoons yellow curry paste
- 1 tablespoon minced fresh ginger
- 1 tablespoon minced garlic
- 1 teaspoon kosher salt
- 1 pound (454 g) boneless, skinless chicken thighs, halved crosswise
- 2 tablespoons chopped peanuts

**Directions:**

1. In a large bowl, stir together the coconut milk, curry paste, ginger, garlic, and salt until well blended. Add the chicken; toss well to coat. Marinate at room temperature for 30 minutes, or cover and refrigerate for up to 24 hours.
2. Preheat the air fryer to 375ºF (191ºC).
3. Place the chicken (along with marinade) in a baking pan. Place the pan in the air fryer basket. Bake for 20 minutes, turning the chicken halfway through the cooking time. Use a meat thermometer to ensure the chicken has reached an internal temperature of 165ºF (74ºC).
4. Sprinkle the chicken with the chopped peanuts and serve.

## Grilled Curried Chicken Wings

Servings: 4

Cooking Time: 35 Minutes

**Ingredients:**

- ½ cup plain yogurt
- 1 tablespoon curry powder
- 2 pounds chicken wings
- Salt and pepper to taste

**Directions:**

1. To season, rub curry powder, salt, yogurt, and pepper over the chicken wings. Toss well to season.
2. Refrigerate the seasoned chicken wings for at least 2 hours.
3. Before cooking, hear your air fryer to 390 degrees F/ 200 degrees C.
4. When ready, transfer the marinated chicken wings onto a grill pan that fits your air fryer.
5. Grill in the preheated air fryer for 35 minutes and flip halfway through cooking to cook evenly.
6. Serve and enjoy!

# Crispy Chicken Nuggets

Servings: 4
Cooking Time: 40 Minutes
**Ingredients:**

- 2 slices bread crumbs
- 9 ounces chicken breast, chopped
- 1 teaspoon garlic, minced
- 1 teaspoon tomato ketchup
- 2 medium eggs

- 1 tablespoon olive oil
- 1 teaspoon. paprika
- 1 teaspoon parsley
- Salt and pepper to taste

**Directions:**

1. To make the batter, combine together the paprika, pepper, salt, oil, and breadcrumbs.
2. Whisk one egg in a separate bowl.
3. Whisk the egg, with ketchup and parsley over the chopped chicken and press to coat well.
4. Make several nuggets from the chicken mixture and dip each in the egg.
5. Then coat the chicken with breadcrumbs.
6. Cook the breaded chicken in your air fryer at 390 degrees F/ 200 degrees C for 10 minutes.
7. If desired, serve the chicken nuggets with your favorite sauce.

# Healthy Chicken With Veggies

Servings: 4 Servings
Cooking Time: 20 Minutes
**Ingredients:**

- 1 pound of chopped chicken breast
- 1 chopped zucchini
- 1 cup of broccoli florets
- 1 cup of chopped bell peppers
- ½ chopped onion
- 2 minced garlic cloves
- 2 tablespoons of olive oil
- 1 tablespoon of Italian seasonings
- ½ teaspoon of garlic powder
- ½ teaspoon of chili powder (optional)
- Pinch of salt and black pepper, to taste

**Directions:**

1. Preheat your air fryer to 400°F.
2. Put the chopped vegetables with chicken breast into a large mixing bowl. Add seasonings with oil and mix it well.
3. Transfer all the ingredients into the air fry basket and cook at 400°F for 10 minutes. Toss halfway through cooking. If it's not ready, cook for 3–5 minutes more.
4. Serve warm and enjoy your Healthy Chicken with Veggies!

# Seasoned Turkey Meat With Kale

Servings: 4
Cooking Time: 15 Minutes
**Ingredients:**

- ½ teaspoon garlic powder
- ½ teaspoon onion powder
- 1 cup coconut milk
- 1-pound leftover turkey, shredded
- 2 cups kale, chopped
- 4 eggs, beaten
- Black pepper and salt to taste

**Directions:**

1. In a suitable mixing bowl, combine the eggs, coconut milk, garlic powder, and onion powder. Season the mixture with black pepper and salt to taste.
2. Place the turkey meat and kale in a suitable baking dish.
3. Pour over the egg mixture.
4. Place in the preheated air fryer.
5. Cook for 15 minutes at 350 degrees F/ 175 degrees C.
6. When done, serve and enjoy.

# Spicy And Crispy Duck

Servings: 3
Cooking Time: 20 Minutes
**Ingredients:**

- 2 tablespoons peanuts, chopped
- 1 tablespoon honey
- 1 tablespoon olive oil
- 1 tablespoon hoisin sauce
- 1 pound duck breast
- 1 small-sized white onion, sliced
- 1 teaspoon garlic, chopped
- 1 celery stick, diced
- 1 thumb ginger, sliced
- 4 baby potatoes, diced

**Directions:**

1. Using cooking oil, lightly grease the air fryer basket.
2. In a mixing bowl, combine honey, hoisin sauce, peanuts, and olive oil.
3. Rub the duck breast with mixture and transfer to the air fryer basket.
4. Spread garlic, celery, potatoes, ginger and onion over the duck breast.
5. Cook at 400 degrees F/ 205 degrees C for 20 minutes.
6. Serve the duck breast with Mandarin pancakes.

# Orange Chicken

Servings: 2 Servings
Cooking Time: 20 Minutes

**Ingredients:**

- 1 pound of chopped chicken breast
- 2 tablespoons of cornstarch + 2 teaspoons for the sauce
- ½ cup of orange juice
- 2 tablespoons of sugar
- 1 tablespoon of vinegar
- 1 tablespoon of soy sauce
- ¼ teaspoon of ground ginger
- Zest of 1 orange
- Dash of red pepper flakes
- Pinch of salt and black pepper, to taste

**Directions:**

1. Preheat your air fryer to 400°F.

2. Add chicken pieces with 2 tablespoons of cornstarch in a bowl and mix well until they are fully coated. Cook them in the air fryer at 400°F for 7–9 minutes. Toss halfway through cooking.

3. Meanwhile, mix sugar, orange juice, soy sauce, vinegar, red pepper flakes, orange zest, and ginger in a small saucepan. Put on medium heat and simmer for 5 minutes.

4. Combine 2 teaspoons of cornstarch with 2 teaspoons of water in a small bowl. Pour the prepared mixture into the orange sauce. Continue simmering for 1 more minute. Remove from the heat.

5. Take the cooked chicken from the air fryer and mix it with sauce.

6. Serve warm* and enjoy your Orange Chicken!

# Garlic Chicken With Bacon

Servings: 2

Cooking Time: 15 Minutes

**Ingredients:**

- 4 rashers smoked bacon
- 2 chicken filets
- ½ teaspoon coarse sea salt
- ¼ teaspoon black pepper, preferably freshly ground
- 1 teaspoon garlic, minced
- 1 (2-inch) piece ginger, peeled and minced
- 1 teaspoon. black mustard seeds
- 1 teaspoon mild curry powder
- ½ cup coconut milk
- ½ cup parmesan cheese, grated

**Directions:**

1. Before cooking, heat your air fryer to 400 degrees F/ 205 degrees C.
2. In the air fryer basket, place the smoked bacon.
3. Cook in your air fryer for 5 to 7 minutes. Set aside for later use.
4. Add the salt, chicken fillets, garlic, mustard seed, milk, curry powder, black pepper, and ginger in a mixing dish.
5. Refrigerate for about 30 minutes to make the marinate.
6. Add the grated parmesan cheese in a second separate bowl.
7. Then dip the parmesan bowl and coat well. Place in the air fryer basket. Decrease the air fryer to 380 degrees F/ 195 degrees C and set the timer for 6 minutes. Start to cook.
8. When the cooking time is up, flip and cook again for 6 minutes.
9. Repeat the prepare cooking steps for the remaining ingredients.
10. Serve with the cooked bacon.

# Spicy Chicken Stir-fry

Servings:4
Cooking Time: 13 To 16 Minutes

**Ingredients:**

- 2 boneless, skinless chicken breasts
- 2 tablespoons cornstarch
- 2 tablespoons peanut oil
- 1 onion, sliced
- 1 jalapeño pepper, sliced
- 1 red bell pepper, chopped
- 1 cup frozen corn
- ½ cup salsa

**Directions:**

1. Cut the chicken breasts into 1-inch cubes. Put the cornstarch on a shallow plate and toss the chicken in it to coat. Set the chicken aside.
2. In a 6-inch metal bowl, combine the oil and onion. Cook for 2 to 3 minutes or until crisp and tender.
3. Add the chicken to the bowl. Cook for 7 to 8 minutes or until almost cooked. Stir in the jalapeño pepper, red bell pepper, corn, and salsa.
4. Cook for 4 to 5 minutes or until the chicken is cooked to 165°F and the vegetables are crisp and tender. Serve over hot rice.

# Rotisserie Whole Chicken

Servings: 6 Servings
Cooking Time: 1 Hour 5 Minutes

**Ingredients:**

- 1 whole chicken without giblets (about 5 pounds)
- 1 tablespoon of salt
- 1 teaspoon of garlic powder
- 1 teaspoon of black pepper
- 1 teaspoon of smoked paprika
- ½ teaspoon of dried oregano
- ½ teaspoon of dried basil
- ½ teaspoon of dried thyme
- 2 tablespoons of olive oil

**Directions:**

1. Preheat your air fryer to 360°F.
2. Mix all seasonings with oil in a mixing bowl and spread it over the chicken.
3. Spray the air fryer basket with cooking spray. Put the chicken breast-side down in the air fryer basket and cook for 50 minutes. Flip it and cook at 360°F for 10 minutes more. If chicken is not 165°F internally, cook for additional 5–10 minutes.
4. Serve warm and enjoy your Rotisserie Whole Chicken!

# Za'atar Chives Chicken With Lemon Zest

Servings: 4
Cooking Time: 18 Minutes
**Ingredients:**

- 1-pound chicken drumsticks, bone-in
- 1 tablespoon za'atar
- 1 teaspoon garlic powder
- ½ teaspoon lemon zest, grated
- 1 teaspoon chives, chopped
- 1 tablespoon avocado oil

**Directions:**

1. In the mixing bowl mix up za'atar, garlic powder, lemon zest, chives, and avocado oil.
2. Then rub the chicken drumsticks with the za'atar mixture.
3. At 375 degrees F/ 190 degrees C, heat your air fryer in advance.
4. Put the prepared chicken drumsticks in the air fryer basket and cook for 15 minutes.
5. Then flip the drumsticks on another side and cook them for 3 minutes more.
6. Serve.

# Chicken Burgers With Ham And Cheese

Servings:4
Cooking Time: 13 To 16 Minutes
**Ingredients:**

- ⅓ cup soft bread crumbs
- 3 tablespoons milk
- 1 egg, beaten
- ½ teaspoon dried thyme
- Pinch salt
- Freshly ground black pepper, to taste
- 1¼ pounds (567 g) ground chicken
- ¼ cup finely chopped ham
- ⅓ cup grated Havarti cheese
- Olive oil for misting

**Directions:**

1. Preheat the air fryer to 350ºF (177ºC).
2. In a medium bowl, combine the bread crumbs, milk, egg, thyme, salt, and pepper. Add the chicken and mix gently but thoroughly with clean hands.
3. Form the chicken into eight thin patties and place on waxed paper.
4. Top four of the patties with the ham and cheese. Top with remaining four patties and gently press the edges together to seal, so the ham and cheese mixture is in the middle of the burger.
5. Place the burgers in the basket and mist with olive oil. Bake for 13 to 16 minutes or until the chicken is thoroughly cooked to 165ºF (74ºC) as measured with a meat thermometer. Serve immediately.

# Buffalo Chicken Taquitos

Servings:6
Cooking Time: 10 Minutes
**Ingredients:**

- Olive oil
- 8 ounces fat-free cream cheese, softened
- ⅛ cup Buffalo sauce
- 2 cups shredded cooked chicken
- 12 (7-inch) low-carb flour tortillas

**Directions:**

1. Spray a fryer basket lightly with olive oil.
2. In a large bowl, mix together the cream cheese and Buffalo sauce until well-combined. Add the chicken and stir until combined.
3. Place the tortillas on a clean workspace. Spoon 2 to 3 tablespoons of the chicken mixture in a thin line down the center of each tortilla. Roll up the tortillas.
4. Place the tortillas in the fryer basket, seam side down. Spray each tortilla lightly with olive oil. You may need to cook the taquitos in batches.
5. Air fry until golden brown, 5 to 10 minutes.

# Barbecue Chicken

Servings:4
Cooking Time: 18 To 20 Minutes
**Ingredients:**

- ⅓ cup no-salt-added tomato sauce
- 2 tablespoons low-sodium grainy mustard
- 2 tablespoons apple cider vinegar
- 1 tablespoon honey
- 2 garlic cloves, minced
- 1 jalapeño pepper, minced
- 3 tablespoons minced onion
- 4 (5-ounce / 142-g) low-sodium boneless, skinless chicken breasts

**Directions:**

1. Preheat the air fryer to 370°F (188°C).
2. In a small bowl, stir together the tomato sauce, mustard, cider vinegar, honey, garlic, jalapeño, and onion.
3. Brush the chicken breasts with some sauce and air fry for 10 minutes.
4. Remove the air fryer basket and turn the chicken; brush with more sauce. Air fry for 5 minutes more.
5. Remove the air fryer basket and turn the chicken again; brush with more sauce. Air fry for 3 to 5 minutes more, or until the chicken reaches an internal temperature of 165°F (74°C) on a meat thermometer. Discard any remaining sauce. Serve immediately.

# Sweet Marinated Chicken Wings

Servings: 6-8
Cooking Time: 12 Minutes
**Ingredients:**

- 16 chicken wings
- To make the marinade:
- 2 tablespoons honey
- 2 tablespoons light soya sauce

- ½ teaspoon sea salt
- ¼ teaspoon black pepper
- ¼ teaspoon white pepper, ground
- 2 tablespoons lemon juice

**Directions:**

1. To marinate, combine the marinade ingredients with the chicken wings in the zip-log bag. Then seal and refrigerate for 4 to 6 minutes.
2. On a flat kitchen surface, plug your air fryer and turn it on.
3. Before cooking, heat the air fryer to 355 degrees F/ 180 degrees C for 4 to 5 minutes.
4. Gently coat the air fryer basket with cooking oil or spray.
5. Place the chicken wings inside the air fryer basket. Cook in your air fryer for 5 to 6 minutes.
6. When cooked, remove the air fryer basket from the air fryer and serve warm with lemon wedges as you like.

# Chicken Tenders With Italian Seasoning

Servings: 2
Cooking Time: 10 Minutes
**Ingredients:**

- 2 eggs, lightly beaten
- 1 ½ pounds chicken tenders
- ½ teaspoon onion powder
- ½ teaspoon garlic powder
- 1 teaspoon paprika
- 1 teaspoon Italian seasoning
- 2 tablespoons' ground flax seed
- 1 cup almond flour
- ½ teaspoon black pepper
- 1 teaspoon salt

**Directions:**

1. At 400 degrees F/ 205 degrees C, preheat your Air fryer.
2. Season chicken with black pepper and salt.
3. In a suitable bowl, whisk eggs to combine.
4. In a shallow dish, mix together almond flour, all seasonings, and flaxseed.
5. Dip chicken into the egg then coats with almond flour mixture and place on a plate.
6. Grease its air fryer basket with cooking spray.
7. Place ½ chicken tenders in air fryer basket and cook for almost 10 minutes, turning halfway through.
8. Cook remaining chicken tenders using same steps.
9. Serve and enjoy.

# Spice Chicken With Broccoli

Servings: 4

Cooking Time: 20 Minutes

**Ingredients:**

- 1-pound chicken breast, boneless, and cut into chunks
- 2 cups broccoli florets
- 2 teaspoons hot sauce
- 2 teaspoons vinegar
- 1 teaspoon sesame oil
- 1 tablespoon soy sauce
- 1 tablespoon ginger, minced
- ½ teaspoon garlic powder
- 1 tablespoon olive oil
- ½ onion, sliced
- Black pepper
- Salt

**Directions:**

1. Add all the recipe ingredients into the suitable mixing bowl and toss well.
2. Grease its air fryer basket with cooking spray.
3. Transfer chicken and broccoli mixture into the air fryer basket.
4. Cook at almost 380 degrees F/ 195 degrees C for almost 15-20 minutes. Shake halfway through.
5. Serve and enjoy.

# Parmesan-lemon Chicken

Servings:4

Cooking Time: 20 Minutes

**Ingredients:**

- 1 egg
- 2 tablespoons lemon juice
- 2 teaspoons minced garlic
- ½ teaspoon salt
- ½ teaspoon freshly ground black pepper
- 4 boneless, skinless chicken breasts, thin cut
- Olive oil
- ½ cup whole-wheat bread crumbs
- ¼ cup grated Parmesan cheese

**Directions:**

1. In a medium bowl, whisk together the egg, lemon juice, garlic, salt, and pepper. Add the chicken breasts, cover, and refrigerate for up to 1 hour.
2. In a shallow bowl, combine the bread crumbs and Parmesan cheese.
3. Spray a fryer basket lightly with olive oil.
4. Remove the chicken breasts from the egg mixture, then dredge them in the bread crumb mixture, and place in the fryer basket in a single layer. Lightly spray the chicken breasts with olive oil. You may need to cook the chicken in batches.
5. Air fry for 8 minutes. Flip the chicken over, lightly spray with olive oil, and cook until the chicken reaches an internal temperature of 165°F, for an additional 7 to 12 minutes.

# Rosemary Chicken With Lemon Wedges

Servings: 2

Cooking Time: 25 Minutes

**Ingredients:**

- ¾ pound chicken
- ½ tablespoon olive oil
- 1 tablespoon soy sauce
- 1 teaspoon fresh ginger, minced
- 1 tablespoon oyster sauce
- 3 tablespoons sugar
- 1 tablespoon fresh rosemary, chopped
- ½ fresh lemon, cut into wedges

**Directions:**

1. In a suitable bowl, combine the chicken, oil, soy sauce, and ginger, coating the chicken well.
2. Refrigerate for 30 minutes.
3. At 390 degrees F/ 200 degrees C, preheat your Air Fryer for 3 minutes.
4. Place the chicken in the baking pan, transfer to the air fryer and cook for 6 minutes.
5. In the meantime, put the rosemary, sugar, and oyster sauce in a suitable bowl and mix together.
6. Add the rosemary mixture in the air fryer over the chicken and top the chicken with the lemon wedges.
7. Resume cooking for another 13 minutes, turning the chicken halfway through.
8. Serve.

# Turkey Breast With Fresh Herbs

Servings: 4

Cooking Time: 35 Minutes

**Ingredients:**

- 2 pounds' turkey breast
- 1 teaspoon fresh sage, chopped
- 1 teaspoon fresh rosemary, chopped
- 1 teaspoon fresh thyme, chopped
- Black pepper
- Salt

**Directions:**

1. Grease its air fryer basket with cooking spray.
2. In a suitable bowl, mix together sage, rosemary, and thyme.
3. Season turkey breast with black pepper and salt and herb mixture.
4. Set the seasoned turkey breast in air fryer basket and cook at almost 390 degrees F/ 200 degrees C for 30-35 minutes.
5. Slice and serve.

# Herbs Chicken Drumsticks With Tamari Sauce

Servings: 6
Cooking Time: 35 Minutes
**Ingredients:**

- 6 chicken drumsticks
- Sauce:
- 6 oz. hot sauce
- 3 tablespoons olive oil
- 3 tablespoons tamari sauce
- 1 teaspoon dried thyme
- ½ teaspoon dried oregano

**Directions:**

1. Spritz a nonstick cooking spray over the sides and bottom of the cooking basket.
2. Cook the chicken drumsticks at 380 degrees F/ 195 degrees C for 35 minutes, flipping them over halfway through.
3. Meanwhile, heat the hot sauce, olive oil, tamari sauce, thyme, and oregano in a pan over medium-low heat; reserve.
4. Drizzle the sauce over the prepared chicken drumsticks; toss to coat well and serve.

# Beef, Pork & Lamb Recipes
## Spice Meatloaf

Servings: 8
Cooking Time: 20 Minutes
**Ingredients:**

- 1-pound ground beef
- ½ teaspoon dried tarragon
- 1 teaspoon Italian seasoning
- 1 tablespoon Worcestershire sauce
- ¼ cup ketchup
- ¼ cup coconut flour
- ½ cup almond flour
- 1 garlic clove, minced
- ¼ cup onion, chopped
- 2 eggs, lightly beaten
- ¼ teaspoon black pepper
- ½ teaspoon salt

**Directions:**

1. Add all the recipe ingredients into the mixing bowl and mix until well combined.
2. Make the equal shape of patties from mixture and place on a plate. Place in refrigerator for 10 minutes.
3. Grease its air fryer basket with cooking spray.
4. At 360 degrees F/ 180 degrees C, preheat your air fryer.
5. Place prepared patties in air fryer basket and cook for 10 minutes.
6. Serve and enjoy.

# Lamb Meatballs

Servings:4

Cooking Time: 8 Minutes

**Ingredients:**

- Meatballs:
- ½ small onion, finely diced
- 1 clove garlic, minced
- 1 pound (454 g) ground lamb
- 2 tablespoons fresh parsley, finely chopped (plus more for garnish)
- 2 teaspoons fresh oregano, finely chopped
- 2 tablespoons milk
- 1 egg yolk
- Salt and freshly ground black pepper, to taste
- ½ cup crumbled feta cheese, for garnish
- Tomato Sauce:
- 2 tablespoons butter
- 1 clove garlic, smashed
- Pinch crushed red pepper flakes
- ¼ teaspoon ground cinnamon
- 1 (28-ounce / 794-g) can crushed tomatoes
- Salt, to taste
- Olive oil, for greasing

**Directions:**

1. Combine all ingredients for the meatballs in a large bowl and mix just until everything is combined. Shape the mixture into 1½-inch balls or shape the meat between two spoons to make quenelles.

2. Preheat the air fryer to 400ºF (204ºC).

3. While the air fryer is preheating, start the quick tomato sauce. Put the butter, garlic and red pepper flakes in a sauté pan and heat over medium heat on the stovetop. Let the garlic sizzle a little, but before the butter browns, add the cinnamon and tomatoes. Bring to a simmer and simmer for 15 minutes. Season with salt.

4. Grease the bottom of the air fryer basket with olive oil and transfer the meatballs to the air fryer basket in one layer, air frying in batches if necessary.

5. Air fry for 8 minutes, giving the basket a shake once during the cooking process to turn the meatballs over.

6. To serve, spoon a pool of the tomato sauce onto plates and add the meatballs. Sprinkle the feta cheese on top and garnish with more fresh parsley. Serve immediately.

# Steak With Onion And Bell Peppers

Servings: 6
Cooking Time: 15 Minutes
**Ingredients:**

- 1 lb. steak, sliced
- 1 tablespoon olive oil
- 1 tablespoon fajita seasoning, gluten-free
- ½ cup onion, sliced
- 3 bell peppers, sliced

**Directions:**

1. Line up the aluminum foil on the cooking basket of your air fryer.
2. In a large bowl, mix up all of the ingredients and toss well until coated.
3. Arrange the fajita mixture to the basket and cook at 390 degrees F/ 200 degrees C for 5 minutes.
4. After 5 minutes, toss well again and cook for 5-10 minutes more.
5. Serve and enjoy.

# Pork Tenderloin With Bell Pepper

Servings: 2
Cooking Time: 18 Minutes
**Ingredients:**

- 1 red onion, make thin slices
- 1 yellow or red bell pepper, make thin strips
- 2 teaspoons herbs
- 1 tablespoon olive oil
- ½ tablespoon mustard
- Black pepper, ground as required
- 11-ounce pork tenderloin

**Directions:**

1. Make the tenderloin into four pieces, spread the oil, mustard and sprinkle some pepper and salt on them.
2. Thoroughly mix the herbs, pepper strips, oil, onion, salt and pepper in a medium-size bowl.
3. Coat the cooking basket of your air fryer with cooking oil or spray.
4. Add the mixture on the basket, put the tenderloin pieces on and then arrange the basket to the air fryer.
5. Cook the tenderloin pieces at 390 degrees F/ 200 degrees C for 16-18 minutes.
6. When done, serve warm!

# Garlic Pork Roast

Servings: 8
Cooking Time: 30 Minutes
**Ingredients:**

- 2 lbs. pork roast
- 1 ½-teaspoon garlic powder
- 1 ½-teaspoon coriander powder
- ⅓-teaspoon salt
- 1 ½-teaspoon black pepper
- 1 ½ dried thyme
- 1 ½-teaspoon dried oregano
- 1 ½-teaspoon cumin powder
- 3 cups water
- 1 lemon, halved

**Directions:**

1. Mix up the garlic powder, coriander powder, salt, black pepper, thyme, oregano and cumin powder in a suitable bowl.
2. Dry the pork well and then poke holes all around it using a fork.
3. Smear the oregano rub thoroughly on all sides with your hands and squeeze the lemon juice all over it. Set aside for 5 minutes.
4. Cook the pork at 300 degrees F/ 150 degrees C for 10 minutes.
5. Turn the pork and increase the temperature to 350 F and continue cooking for 10 minutes.
6. Once ready, remove it and place it in on a chopping board to sit for 4 minutes before slicing. Serve the pork slices with a side of sautéed asparagus and hot sauce.

# Teriyaki Pork And Mushroom Rolls

Servings:6
Cooking Time: 8 Minutes
**Ingredients:**

- 4 tablespoons brown sugar
- 4 tablespoons mirin
- 4 tablespoons soy sauce
- 1 teaspoon almond flour
- 2-inch ginger, chopped
- 6 (4-ounce / 113-g) pork belly slices
- 6 ounces (170 g) Enoki mushrooms

**Directions:**

1. Mix the brown sugar, mirin, soy sauce, almond flour, and ginger together until brown sugar dissolves.
2. Take pork belly slices and wrap around a bundle of mushrooms. Brush each roll with teriyaki sauce. Chill for half an hour.
3. Preheat the air fryer to 350ºF (177ºC) and add marinated pork rolls.
4. Air fry for 8 minutes. Flip the rolls halfway through.
5. Serve immediately.

# Peppercorn Crusted Beef Tenderloin

Servings:6

Cooking Time: 25 Minutes

**Ingredients:**

- 2 pounds (907 g) beef tenderloin
- 2 teaspoons roasted garlic, minced
- 2 tablespoons salted butter, melted
- 3 tablespoons ground 4-peppercorn blender

**Directions:**

1. Preheat the air fryer to 400ºF (204ºC).
2. Remove any surplus fat from the beef tenderloin.
3. Combine the roasted garlic and melted butter to apply to the tenderloin with a brush.
4. On a plate, spread out the peppercorns and roll the tenderloin in them, making sure they are covering and clinging to the meat.
5. Air fry the tenderloin in the air fryer for 25 minutes, turning halfway through cooking.
6. Let the tenderloin rest for ten minutes before slicing and serving.

# Beef Ribeye Steak

Servings: 4

Cooking Time: 20 Minutes

**Ingredients:**

- 4 (8-ounce) ribeye steaks
- 1 tablespoon McCormick Grill Mates Montreal Steak Seasoning
- Salt
- Pepper

**Directions:**

1. Season the steaks with the steak seasoning and salt and pepper to taste.
2. Place 2 steaks in the air fryer. You can use an accessory grill pan, a layer rack, or the standard air fryer basket. Cook for 4 minutes.
3. Open the air fryer and flip the steaks. Cook for an additional 4 to 5 minutes.
4. Check for doneness to determine how much additional cook time is need. (See Cooking tip.)
5. Remove the cooked steaks from the air fryer, then repeat steps 2 through 4 for the remaining 2 steaks.
6. Cool before serving.

# Chicken-fried Steak

Servings:4
Cooking Time: 15 Minutes
**Ingredients:**

- 4 (6-ounce) beef cube steaks
- ½ cup buttermilk
- 1 cup flour
- 2 teaspoons paprika
- 1 teaspoon garlic salt
- 1 egg
- 1 cup soft bread crumbs
- 2 tablespoons olive oil

**Directions:**

1.  Place the cube steaks on a plate or cutting board and gently pound until they are slightly thinner. Set aside.
2.  In a shallow bowl, combine the buttermilk, flour, paprika, garlic salt, and egg until just combined.
3.  On a plate, combine the bread crumbs and olive oil and mix well.
4.  Dip the steaks into the buttermilk batter to coat, and let sit on a plate for 5 minutes.
5.  Dredge the steaks in the bread crumbs. Pat the crumbs onto both sides to coat the steaks thoroughly.
6.  Air-fry the steaks for 12 to 16 minutes or until the meat reaches 160°F on a meat thermometer and the coating is brown and crisp. You can serve this with heated beef gravy.
7.  Did You Know? Cube steaks have been "mechanically tenderized" and have to be cooked to well done. The meat has been pierced with needles or blades to cut up the fibers in the meat so it will be tender when cooked. This also means that bacteria on the surface of the meat have been pushed through to the inside. For safety reasons, cook this type of steak to 160°F.

# Bacon Garlic Pizza

Servings:4
Cooking Time: 20 Minutes
**Ingredients:**

- Flour, for dusting
- Nonstick baking spray with flour
- 4 frozen large whole-wheat dinner rolls, thawed
- 5 cloves garlic, minced
- ¾ cup pizza sauce
- ½ teaspoon dried oregano
- ½ teaspoon garlic salt
- 8 slices precooked bacon, cut into 1-inch pieces
- 1¼ cups shredded Cheddar cheese

**Directions:**

1. On a lightly floured surface, press out each dinner roll to a 5-by-3-inch oval.
2. Spray four 6-by-4-inch pieces of heavy duty foil with nonstick spray and place one crust on each piece.
3. Bake, two at a time, for 2 minutes or until the crusts are set, but not browned.
4. Meanwhile, in a small bowl, combine the garlic, pizza sauce, oregano, and garlic salt. When the pizza crusts are set, spread each with some of the sauce. Top with the bacon pieces and Cheddar cheese.
5. Bake, two at a time, for another 8 minutes or until the crust is browned and the cheese is melted and starting to brown.

# Elegant Pork Chops

Servings: 4
Cooking Time: 25 Minutes
**Ingredients:**

- 4 pork chops, bone-in
- Salt and black pepper, to taste
- ½ teaspoon onion powder
- ½ teaspoon paprika
- ½ teaspoon celery seeds
- 2 cooking apples, peeled and sliced
- 1 tablespoon honey
- 1 tablespoon peanut oil

**Directions:**

1. Place the pork in a suitable greased baking pan.
2. Season with black pepper and salt, and transfer the pan to the cooking basket.
3. Cook the pork chops in the preheated air fryer at about 370 degrees F/ 185 degrees C for almost 10 minutes.
4. Meanwhile, in a suitable saucepan, simmer the remaining ingredients over medium heat for about 8 minutes or until the apples are softened.
5. Pour the applesauce over the prepared pork chops.
6. Add to the preheated Air Fryer and air fry for 5 minutes more.

# Pork And Pinto Bean Gorditas

Servings:4
Cooking Time: 21 Minutes

**Ingredients:**

- 1 pound (454 g) lean ground pork
- 2 tablespoons chili powder
- 2 tablespoons ground cumin
- 1 teaspoon dried oregano
- 2 teaspoons paprika
- 1 teaspoon garlic powder
- ½ cup water
- 1 (15-ounce / 425-g) can pinto beans, drained and rinsed
- ½ cup taco sauce
- Salt and freshly ground black pepper, to taste
- 2 cups grated Cheddar cheese
- 5 (12-inch) flour tortillas
- 4 (8-inch) crispy corn tortilla shells
- 4 cups shredded lettuce
- 1 tomato, diced
- ⅓ cup sliced black olives
- Sour cream, for serving
- Tomato salsa, for serving
- Cooking spray

**Directions:**

1.  Preheat the air fryer to 400ºF (204ºC). Spritz the air fryer basket with cooking spray.

2.  Put the ground pork in the air fryer basket and air fry at 400ºF (204ºC) for 10 minutes, stirring a few times to gently break up the meat. Combine the chili powder, cumin, oregano, paprika, garlic powder and water in a small bowl. Stir the spice mixture into the browned pork. Stir in the beans and taco sauce and air fry for an additional minute. Transfer the pork mixture to a bowl. Season with salt and freshly ground black pepper.

3.  Sprinkle ½ cup of the grated cheese in the center of the flour tortillas, leaving a 2-inch border around the edge free of cheese and filling. Divide the pork mixture among the four tortillas, placing it on top of the cheese. Put a crunchy corn tortilla on top of the pork and top with shredded lettuce, diced tomatoes, and black olives. Cut the remaining flour tortilla into 4 quarters. These quarters of tortilla will serve as the bottom of the gordita. Put one quarter tortilla on top of each gordita and fold the edges of the bottom flour tortilla up over the sides, enclosing the filling. While holding the seams down, brush the bottom of the gordita with olive oil and place the seam side down on the countertop while you finish the remaining three gorditas.

4.  Preheat the air fryer to 380ºF (193ºC).

5.  Air fry one gordita at a time. Transfer the gordita carefully to the air fryer basket, seam side down. Brush or spray the top tortilla with oil and air fry for 5 minutes. Carefully turn the gordita over and air fry for an additional 4 to 5 minutes until both sides are browned. When finished air frying all four gorditas, layer them back into the air fryer for an additional minute to make sure they are all warm before serving with sour cream and salsa.

6.  Serve

# Spicy Pork Belly Pieces

Servings: 4
Cooking Time: 50 Minutes
**Ingredients:**

- 1 ½ lbs. pork belly, cut into 4 pieces
- Kosher salt and ground black pepper, to taste
- 1 teaspoon smoked paprika
- ½-teaspoon turmeric powder
- 1 tablespoon oyster sauce
- 1 tablespoon green onions
- 4 cloves garlic, sliced
- 1 lb. new potatoes, scrubbed

**Directions:**

1. Heat your Air Fryer to 390 degrees F/ 200 degrees C in advance.
2. Use the kitchen to pat the pork belly pieces dry and season with the remaining spices.
3. Spray the coated pieces with a non-stick spray on all sides and add the oyster sauce.
4. Cook the pork belly pieces in the preheated Air Fryer for 30 minutes.
5. Turn them over every 10 minutes.
6. When the time is over, increase the temperature to 400 degrees F/ 205 degrees C.
7. Add the green onions, garlic, and new potatoes and cook for another 15 minutes, shaking regularly.
8. When done, serve warm and enjoy.

# Breaded Italian Pork Chops

Servings:4
Cooking Time: 15 Minutes
**Ingredients:**

- Olive oil
- 2 eggs, beaten
- ¼ cup whole-wheat bread crumbs
- 1 envelope zesty Italian dressing mix
- 4 thin boneless pork chops, trimmed of excess fat
- Salt
- Freshly ground black pepper

**Directions:**

1. Spray a fryer basket lightly with olive oil.
2. Place the eggs in a shallow bowl.
3. In a separate shallow bowl, mix together the bread crumbs and Italian dressing mix.
4. Season the pork chops with salt and pepper. Coat the pork chops in the egg, shaking off any excess. Dredge them in the bread crumb mixture.
5. Place the pork chops in the fryer basket in a single layer and spray lightly with olive oil. You may need to cook them in batches.
6. Air fry for 7 minutes. Flip the pork chops over, lightly spray with olive oil, and cook until they reach an internal temperature of at least 145°F, an additional 5 to 8 minutes.

# Korean Short Ribs

Servings: 4
Cooking Time: 10 Minutes
**Ingredients:**

- 8 (8-ounce) bone-in short ribs
- ½ cup soy sauce
- ¼ cup rice wine vinegar (see Substitution tip)
- ½ cup chopped onion
- 2 garlic cloves, minced
- 1 tablespoon sesame oil
- 1 teaspoon Sriracha
- 4 scallions, green parts (white parts optional), thinly sliced, divided
- Salt
- Pepper

**Directions:**

1. Place the short ribs in a sealable plastic bag. Add the soy sauce, rice wine vinegar, onion, garlic, sesame oil, Sriracha, and half of the scallions. Season with salt and pepper to taste.
2. Seal the bag and place it in the refrigerator to marinate for at least 1 hour; overnight is optimal.
3. Place the short ribs in the air fryer. Do not overfill. You may have to cook in two batches. Cook for 4 minutes.
4. Open the air fryer and flip the ribs. Cook for an additional 4 minutes.
5. If necessary, remove the cooked short ribs from the air fryer, then repeat steps 3 and 4 for the remaining ribs.
6. Sprinkle the short ribs with the remaining scallions, and serve.

# Porterhouse Steak With Mustard And Butter

Servings: 2
Cooking Time: 15 Minutes
**Ingredients:**

- 1 lb. porterhouse steak, cut meat from bone in 2 pieces
- ½-teaspoon ground black pepper
- ½ teaspoon cayenne pepper
- ½-teaspoon salt
- ½ teaspoon garlic powder
- ½-teaspoon dried thyme
- ½-teaspoon dried marjoram
- ½ teaspoon Dijon mustard
- 1 tablespoon butter, melted

**Directions:**

1. Sprinkle all the seasonings on the top of the porterhouse steak.
2. Evenly coat the steak with the mustard and butter.
3. Cook the processed steak at 390 degrees F/ 200 degrees C for 12 to 14 minutes.
4. When done, serve and enjoy.

# Steak Mushroom Bites

Servings: 3
Cooking Time: 18 Minutes
**Ingredients:**

- 1-pound steaks, cut into ½-inch cubes
- ½ teaspoon garlic powder
- 1 teaspoon Worcestershire sauce
- 2 tablespoons butter, melted
- 8 oz. mushrooms, sliced
- Black pepper
- Salt

**Directions:**

1. Add all the recipe ingredients into the suitable mixing bowl and toss well.
2. Grease its air fryer basket with cooking spray.
3. At 400 degrees F/ 205 degrees C, preheat your air fryer.
4. Add steak mushroom mixture into the air fryer basket and cook at almost 400 degrees F/ 205 degrees C for almost 15-18 minutes. Shake basket twice.
5. Serve and enjoy.

# Spiced Beef Chuck Roast

Servings: 6
Cooking Time: 1 Hour
**Ingredients:**

- 1 pound beef chuck roast
- 1 onion, chopped
- 2 cloves of garlic, minced
- 2 tablespoons olive oil
- 3 cups water
- 1 tablespoon butter
- 1 tablespoon Worcestershire sauce
- 1 teaspoon rosemary
- 1 teaspoon thyme
- 3 stalks of celery, sliced

**Directions:**

1. Stir all of the ingredients and arrange them to the cooking pan of your air fryer.
2. Cook them at 350 degrees F/ 175 degrees C for 60 minutes, braising the meat with its sauce halfway through.
3. When done, serve and enjoy.

# Sumptuous Pizza Tortilla Rolls

Servings:4

Cooking Time: 6 Minutes

**Ingredients:**

- 1 teaspoon butter
- ½ medium onion, slivered
- ½ red or green bell pepper, julienned
- 4 ounces (113 g) fresh white mushrooms, chopped
- ½ cup pizza sauce
- 8 flour tortillas
- 8 thin slices deli ham
- 24 pepperoni slices
- 1 cup shredded Mozzarella cheese
- Cooking spray

**Directions:**

1. Preheat the air fryer to 390ºF (199ºC).
2. Put butter, onions, bell pepper, and mushrooms in a baking pan. Bake in the preheated air fryer for 3 minutes. Stir and cook 3 to 4 minutes longer until just crisp and tender. Remove pan and set aside.
3. To assemble rolls, spread about 2 teaspoons of pizza sauce on one half of each tortilla. Top with a slice of ham and 3 slices of pepperoni. Divide sautéed vegetables among tortillas and top with cheese.
4. Roll up tortillas, secure with toothpicks if needed, and spray with oil.
5. Put 4 rolls in air fryer basket and air fry for 4 minutes. Turn and air fry 4 minutes, until heated through and lightly browned.
6. Repeat step 4 to air fry remaining pizza rolls.
7. Serve immediately.

# Polish Beef Sausage With Worcestershire Sauce

Servings: 4

Cooking Time: 11 Minutes

**Ingredients:**

- 1 pound smoked Polish beef sausage, sliced
- 1 tablespoon mustard
- 1 tablespoon olive oil
- 2 tablespoons Worcestershire sauce
- 2 bell peppers, sliced
- 2 cups sourdough bread, cubed
- Salt and black pepper, to taste

**Directions:**

1. Toss the sausage with the mustard, olive, and Worcestershire sauce.
2. Thread sausage, black peppers, and bread onto skewers.
3. Sprinkle with black pepper and salt.
4. Cook in the preheated Air Fryer at about 360 degrees F/ 180 degrees C for 11 minutes.
5. Brush the skewers with the reserved marinade.
6. Serve

# Marinated Pork Tenderloin

Servings:6
Cooking Time: 30 Minutes
**Ingredients:**

- ¼ cup olive oil
- ¼ cup soy sauce
- ¼ cup freshly squeezed lemon juice
- 1 garlic clove, minced

- 1 tablespoon Dijon mustard
- 1 teaspoon salt
- ½ teaspoon freshly ground black pepper
- 2 pounds (907 g) pork tenderloin

**Directions:**

1. In a large mixing bowl, make the marinade: Mix the olive oil, soy sauce, lemon juice, minced garlic, Dijon mustard, salt, and pepper. Reserve ¼ cup of the marinade.
2. Put the tenderloin in a large bowl and pour the remaining marinade over the meat. Cover and marinate in the refrigerator for about 1 hour.
3. Preheat the air fryer to 400ºF (204ºC).
4. Put the marinated pork tenderloin into the air fryer basket. Roast for 10 minutes. Flip the pork and baste it with half of the reserved marinade. Roast for 10 minutes more.
5. Flip the pork, then baste with the remaining marinade. Roast for another 10 minutes, for a total cooking time of 30 minutes.
6. Serve immediately.

# Fish And Seafood Recipes

## Southwestern Prawns With Asparagus

Servings: 3
Cooking Time: 5 Minutes
**Ingredients:**

- 1-pound prawns, deveined
- ½ pound asparagus spears, cut into1-inch chinks
- 1 teaspoon butter, melted
- ¼ teaspoon oregano
- ½ teaspoon mixed peppercorns, crushed
- Salt, to taste
- 1 ripe avocado
- 1 lemon, sliced
- ½ cup chunky-style salsa

**Directions:**

1. Toss your prawns and asparagus with melted butter, oregano, salt and mixed peppercorns.
2. Cook the prawns and asparagus at 400 degrees F/ 205 degrees C for 5 minutes, shaking the air fryer basket halfway through the cooking time.
3. Divide the prawns and asparagus between serving plates and garnish with avocado and lemon slices. Serve with the salsa on the side. Bon appétit!

# Spanish Garlic Shrimp

Servings:4

Cooking Time: 15 Minutes

**Ingredients:**

- 2 teaspoons olive oil plus more for spraying
- 2 teaspoons minced garlic
- 2 teaspoons lemon juice
- ½ to 1 teaspoon crushed red pepper
- 12 ounces medium cooked shrimp, thawed, and deveined, with tails on

**Directions:**

1. Spray a fryer basket lightly with olive oil.
2. In a medium bowl, mix together the garlic, lemon juice, 2 teaspoons of olive oil, and crushed red pepper to make a marinade.
3. Add the shrimp and toss to coat in the marinade. Cover with plastic wrap and place the bowl in the refrigerator for 30 minutes.
4. Place the shrimp in the fryer basket. Air fry for 5 minutes. Shake the basket and cook until the shrimp are cooked through and nicely browned, an additional 5 to 10 minutes.

# Salmon Burgers

Servings: 4

Cooking Time: 15 Minutes

**Ingredients:**

- 1 lb. salmon
- 1 egg
- 1 garlic clove, minced
- 2 green onions, minced
- 1 cup parmesan cheese
- Sauce:
- 1 teaspoon rice wine
- 1 ½-tablespoon soy sauce
- A pinch of salt
- 1 teaspoon gochutgaru (Korean red chili pepper flakes)

**Directions:**

1. Start by preheating your Air Fryer to 380 degrees F/ 195 degrees C. Spritz the Air Fryer basket with cooking oil.
2. Oil the basket of your air fryer.
3. Mix up the salmon with egg, garlic, green onions, and Parmesan cheese in a bowl.
4. Knead it with your hands until everything comes together nicely.
5. Shape the mixture into equally sized patties.
6. Transfer your patties to the basket and arrange the basket to the air fryer.
7. Cook the fish patties for 10 minutes, flipping halfway through.
8. Make the sauce by whisking all ingredients.
9. With the sauce on the side, serve and enjoy the warm fish patties.

# Creamy Savory Salmon

Servings: 4
Cooking Time: 25 Minutes
**Ingredients:**

- For salmon:
- 2 teaspoons olive oil
- 24-ounce (4 pieces) salmon
- 1 pinch salt
- For the sauce:
- ½ cup sour cream
- ½ cup non-fat: Greek yogurt
- 1 pinch salt
- 2 tablespoons dill, finely chopped

**Directions:**

1. Make the salmon pieces of 6 ounces each, brush the pieces with olive oil and then top them with salt.
2. Place the pieces in the basket that has been coated with cooking oil or spray.
3. Arrange the basket to the air fryer and cook at 270 degrees F/ 130 degrees C for 20-25 minutes.
4. In a bowl of medium size, thoroughly mix the sauce ingredients.
5. When the pieces has finished, serve warm with the sauce!


# Country Shrimp "boil"

Servings:4
Cooking Time: 20 Minutes
**Ingredients:**

- 2 tablespoons olive oil, plus more for spraying
- 1 pound large shrimp, deveined, tail on
- 1 pound smoked turkey sausage, cut into thick slices
- 2 corn cobs, quartered
- 1 zucchini, cut into bite-sized pieces
- 1 red bell pepper, cut into chunks
- 1 tablespoon Old Bay seasoning

**Directions:**

1. Spray the fryer basket lightly with olive oil.
2. In a large bowl, mix together the shrimp, turkey sausage, corn, zucchini, bell pepper, and Old Bay seasoning, and toss to coat with the spices. Add the 2 tablespoons of olive oil and toss again until evenly coated.
3. Spread the mixture in the fryer basket in a single layer. You will need to cook in batches.
4. Air fry until cooked through, 15 to 20 minutes, shaking the basket every 5 minutes for even cooking.

# Tilapia Fillets With Mayonnaise

Servings: 4
Cooking Time: 12 Minutes
**Ingredients:**

- 1 tablespoon olive oil, extra-virgin
- 4 tilapia fillets
- Celery salt, as needed
- Freshly cracked pink peppercorns, as needed
- For the Sauce:
- ½ cup crème fraiche
- ¼ cup Cottage cheese
- 2 tablespoons mayonnaise
- 1 tablespoon capers, finely chopped

**Directions:**

1. Thoroughly mix up the olive oil, celery salt, and cracked peppercorns in a medium-sized bowl, then let the fillets be coated with the mixture.
2. Coat the air-frying basket with the cooking oil and spray.
3. Arrange the fillets to the basket and cook for 12 minutes at 360 degrees F/ 180 degrees C.
4. To make a sauce, in a bowl of medium size, thoroughly mix the remaining ingredients to make a sauce.
5. When the time is up, serve warm with the sauce!

# Healthy Salmon With Cardamom

Servings: 2
Cooking Time: 12 Minutes
**Ingredients:**

- 2 salmon fillets
- 1 tablespoon olive oil
- ¼ teaspoon ground cardamom
- ½ teaspoon paprika
- Salt

**Directions:**

1. At 350 degrees F/ 175 degrees C, preheat your air fryer.
2. Coat salmon fillets with paprika, olive oil, cardamom, paprika, and salt and place into the air fryer basket.
3. Cook salmon for almost 10-12 minutes. Turn halfway through.
4. Serve and enjoy.

# Grouper With Miso-honey Sauce

Servings: 2
Cooking Time: 10 Minutes
**Ingredients:**

- ¾ pound grouper fillets
- Salt and white pepper, to taste
- 1 tablespoon sesame oil
- 1 teaspoon water
- 1 teaspoon deli mustard or Dijon mustard
- ¼ cup white miso
- 1 tablespoon mirin
- 1 tablespoon honey
- 1 tablespoon Shoyu sauce

**Directions:**

1. Sprinkle salt and white pepper on the grouper fillets, then drizzle them with a nonstick cooking oil.
2. Arrange the fillets to the air fryer and cook them at 400 degrees F/ 205 degrees C for 10 minutes, flipping halfway through.
3. Meanwhile, whisk the other ingredients to make the sauce.
4. Serve the warm fish with the miso-honey sauce on the side. Bon appétit!

# Haddock Cakes

Servings: 3
Cooking Time: 10 Minutes
**Ingredients:**

- 1 pound haddock
- 1 egg
- 2 tablespoons milk
- 1 bell pepper, deveined and finely chopped
- 2 stalks fresh scallions, minced
- ½ teaspoon fresh garlic, minced
- Sea salt, to taste
- Ground black pepper, to taste
- ½ teaspoon cumin seeds
- ¼ teaspoon celery seeds
- ½ cup breadcrumbs
- 1 teaspoon olive oil

**Directions:**

1. In addition to the breadcrumbs and olive oil, thoroughly combine the other ingredients.
2. Form 3 patties from the mixture and coat them with breadcrumbs, pressing to adhere.
3. Place the patties on the cooking basket and then drizzle the olive oil on them.
4. Arrange the basket to the air fryer and cook at 400 degrees F/ 205 degrees C for 10 minutes, flipping halfway through.
5. Bon appétit!

# Glazed Fillets

Servings: 4
Cooking Time: 15 Minutes
**Ingredients:**

- 4 flounder fillets
- 1 ½ tablespoons dark sesame oil
- 2 tablespoons sake
- Sea salt and cracked mixed peppercorns, as needed
- ¼ cup soy sauce
- 1 teaspoon brown sugar
- 1 tablespoon grated lemon rind
- 2 garlic cloves, minced
- Fresh chopped chives, to serve

**Directions:**

1. To marinate, prepare a large deep dish, add the ingredients except for chives and stir a little. Cover and refrigerate for 2-3 hours.
2. Add the fish to the basket that has been coated with the cooking oil or spray.
3. Arrange it to the air fryer and cook at 360 degrees F/ 180 degrees C for 12 minutes, flipping halfway through.
4. Pour the remaining marinade into a saucepan; simmer over medium-low heat until it has thickened.
5. Serve the fish with the marinade and chives on top!

# Sweet And Sour Glazed Salmon

Servings: 2
Cooking Time: 12 Minutes
**Ingredients:**

- 2 salmon fillets, boneless
- 1 tablespoon honey
- ½ cup blackberries
- 1 tablespoon olive oil
- Juice of ½ lemon
- Black pepper and salt to taste

**Directions:**

1. In a blender, mix the blackberries with the honey, oil, lemon juice, salt, and black pepper; pulse well.
2. Spread the blackberry mixture over the salmon, and then place the fish in your air fryer basket.
3. Cook at almost 380 degrees F/ 195 degrees C for 12 minutes, flipping the fish halfway.
4. Serve hot, and enjoy!

# Lemon Breaded Fish

Servings: 4
Cooking Time: 12 Minutes
**Ingredients:**

- ½ cup breadcrumbs
- 4 tablespoons vegetable oil
- 1 egg
- 4 fish fillets
- 1 lemon

**Directions:**

1. Heat the air fryer to reach 355 degrees F/ 180 degrees C.
2. Whisk the oil and breadcrumbs until crumbly.
3. Dip the prepared fish into the egg, then the crumb mixture.
4. Arrange the fish in the cooker and air-fry for 12 minutes.
5. Garnish using the lemon.

# Air Fried Mussels With Parsley

Servings: 5
Cooking Time: 12 Minutes
**Ingredients:**

- 1 ⅔ pound mussels
- 1 garlic clove
- 1 teaspoon oil
- Black pepper to taste
- Parsley Taste

**Directions:**

1. Clean and scrape the mold cover and remove the byssus.
2. Pour the oil, clean the mussels and the crushed garlic in the air fryer basket.
3. At 425 degrees F/ 220 degrees C, preheat your air fryer and air fry for 12 minutes.
4. Towards the end of cooking, add black pepper and chopped parsley.
5. Finally, distribute the mussel juice well at the bottom of the basket, stirring the basket.

# Beer Squid

Servings: 3
Cooking Time: 20 Minutes
**Ingredients:**

- 1 cup beer
- 1 lb. squid
- 1 cup all-purpose flour
- 2 eggs
- ½ cup cornstarch
- Sea salt, to taste
- ½-teaspoon ground black pepper
- 1 tablespoon Old Bay seasoning

**Directions:**

1. At 390 degrees F/ 200 degrees C, heat your air fryer in advance.
2. Clean the squid and then cut them into rings. Add the beer and squid in a glass bowl, cover and let it sit in your refrigerator for 1 hour.
3. Rinse the squid before patting it dry.
4. Add the flour in a shallow bowl; in another bowl, whisk the eggs. Lastly, in a third shallow bowl, add the cornstarch and seasonings.
5. Dredge the calamari in the flour.
6. Then dip the rings into the egg mixture and coat them with the cornstarch on all sided.
7. Arrange them in the cooking basket. Spritz with cooking oil and cook for 9 to 12 minutes, depending on the desired level of doneness. Work in batches.
8. Serve warm with your favorite dipping sauce. Enjoy!

# Red Snapper With Hot Chili Paste

Servings: 4
Cooking Time: 15 Minutes
**Ingredients:**

- 4 red snapper fillets, boneless
- A pinch of salt and black pepper
- 2 garlic cloves, minced
- 1 tablespoon coconut aminos
- 1 tablespoon lime juice
- 1 tablespoon hot chili paste
- 1 tablespoon olive oil

**Directions:**

1. In addition to the fish, mix up the other ingredients in a bowl and stir well.
2. Use the mixture to rub the fish, then place the fish in the basket of your air fryer.
3. Cook for 15 minutes at 380 degrees F/ 195 degrees C.
4. Serve with a side salad.

# Spicy Orange Shrimp

Servings:4
Cooking Time: 15 Minutes
**Ingredients:**
- Olive oil
- ⅓ cup orange juice
- 3 teaspoons minced garlic
- 1 teaspoon Old Bay seasoning
- ¼ to ½ teaspoon cayenne pepper
- 1 pound medium shrimp, thawed, deveined, peeled, with tails off

**Directions:**
1. Spray a fryer basket lightly with olive oil.
2. In a medium bowl, combine the orange juice, garlic, Old Bay seasoning, and cayenne pepper.
3. Dry the shrimp with paper towels to remove excess water.
4. Add the shrimp to the marinade and stir to evenly coat. Cover with plastic wrap and place in the refrigerator for 30 minutes so the shrimp can soak up the marinade.
5. Place the shrimp into the fryer basket. Air fry for 5 minutes. Shake the basket and lightly spray with olive oil. Cook until the shrimp are opaque and crisp, 5 to 10 more minutes.

# Tex-mex Salmon Stir-fry

Servings: 4
Cooking Time:9 To 14 Minutes
**Ingredients:**
- 12 ounces salmon fillets, cut into 1½-inch cubes (see Tip)
- 1 red bell pepper, chopped
- 1 red onion, chopped
- 1 jalapeño pepper, minced
- ¼ cup low-sodium salsa
- 2 tablespoons low-sodium tomato juice
- 2 teaspoons peanut oil or safflower oil
- 1 teaspoon chili powder
- Brown rice or polenta, cooked (optional)

**Directions:**
1. In a medium metal bowl, stir together the salmon, red bell pepper, red onion, jalapeño, salsa, tomato juice, peanut oil, and chili powder.
2. Place the bowl in the air fryer and cook for 9 to 14 minutes, until the salmon is just cooked through and firm and the vegetables are crisp-tender, stirring once. Serve immediately over hot cooked brown rice or polenta, if desired.

# Delicious Grouper Filets

Servings: 3
Cooking Time: 10 Minutes
**Ingredients:**

- 1 pound grouper filets
- ¼ teaspoon shallot powder
- ¼ teaspoon porcini powder
- 1 teaspoon fresh garlic, minced
- ½ teaspoon cayenne pepper
- ½ teaspoon hot paprika
- ¼ teaspoon oregano
- ½ teaspoon marjoram
- ½ teaspoon sage
- 1 tablespoon butter, melted
- Sea salt and black pepper, to taste

**Directions:**

1. Use the kitchen towels to pat dry the grouper filets.
2. Mix up the remaining ingredients until well incorporated, then rub the grouper filets on all sides with the mixture.
3. Cook the grouper filets in the preheated Air Fryer at 400 degrees F/ 205 degrees C for 10 minutes, flipping halfway through.
4. Serve over hot rice if desired. Bon appétit!

# Baked Sardines

Servings: 3
Cooking Time: 40 Minutes
**Ingredients:**

- 1-pound fresh sardines
- Sea salt, to taste
- Ground black pepper, to taste
- 1 teaspoon Italian seasoning mix
- 2 cloves garlic, minced
- 3 tablespoons olive oil
- ½ lemon, freshly squeezed

**Directions:**

1. Toss salt, black pepper, Italian seasoning mix and the sardines well.
2. Cook the sardines in your air fryer at 325 degrees F/ 160 degrees C for 35 to 40 minutes or until skin is crispy.
3. To make the sauce, whisk the remaining ingredients.
4. Serve warm sardines with the sauce on the side. Bon appétit!

# Ginger-garlic Swordfish

Servings: 3
Cooking Time: 10 Minutes
**Ingredients:**

- 1 pound swordfish steak
- 1 teaspoon ginger-garlic paste
- Sea salt, to taste
- Ground black pepper, to taste
- ¼ teaspoon cayenne pepper
- ¼ teaspoon dried dill weed
- ½ pound mushrooms

**Directions:**

1.  Mix up the ginger-garlic paste; season with salt, black pepper, cayenne pepper and dried dill, then rub the swordfish steak with the mixture.
2.  Spritz the fish with a nonstick cooking spray and transfer to the Air Fryer cooking basket. Cook the swordfish at 400 degrees F/ 205 degrees C for 5 minutes.
3.  Now, add the mushrooms to the cooking basket and continue to cook for 5 minutes longer until tender and fragrant. Eat warm.

# Chunky Fish With Mustard

Servings: 4
Cooking Time: 10 Minutes
**Ingredients:**

- 2 cans canned fish
- 2 celery stalks, trimmed and finely chopped
- 1 egg, whisked
- 1 cup bread crumbs
- 1 teaspoon whole-grain mustard
- ½-teaspoon sea salt
- ¼-teaspoon freshly cracked black peppercorns
- ½ teaspoon paprika

**Directions:**

1.  Add all of the ingredients one by one and combine well.
2.  Form four equal-sized cakes from the mixture, then leave to chill in the refrigerator for 50 minutes.
3.  Spray all sides of each cake after putting them on the cooking pan of your air fryer.
4.  Arrange the pan to the air fryer and grill at 360 degrees F/ 180 degrees C for 5 minutes.
5.  After 5 minutes, turn the cakes over and resume cooking for an additional 3 minutes.
6.  Serve with mashed potatoes if desired.

# Vegetable Side Dishes Recipes

## Crunchy Green Beans

Servings: 4
Cooking Time: 10 Minutes

**Ingredients:**

- 1½ pounds green beans, trimmed
- 1 tablespoon extra-virgin olive oil
- 1 teaspoon garlic powder
- Salt
- Pepper

**Directions:**

1. In a large bowl, drizzle the green beans with the olive oil. Sprinkle with the garlic powder and salt and pepper to taste. Mix well.
2. Transfer the green beans to the air fryer basket. Cook for 4 minutes.
3. Open the air fryer and shake the basket. Cook for an additional 3 to 4 minutes, until the green beans have turned slightly brown.
4. Cool before serving.

## Stuffed Bell Peppers With Mayonnaise

Servings: 2
Cooking Time: 15 Minutes

**Ingredients:**

- 2 red bell peppers, tops and seeds removed
- 2 yellow bell peppers, tops and seeds removed
- Black pepper and salt, to taste
- 1 cup cream cheese
- 4 tablespoons mayonnaise
- 2 pickles, chopped

**Directions:**

1. Arrange the black peppers in the lightly greased cooking basket. Cook in the preheated air fryer at about 400 degrees F/ 205 degrees C for almost 15 minutes, flipping them once halfway through the cooking time.
2. Season with black pepper and salt.
3. Then, in a suitable mixing bowl, combine the cream cheese with the mayonnaise and chopped pickles.
4. Stuff the black pepper with the cream cheese mixture and serve.
5. Enjoy!

# Lemony Cabbage Slaw

Servings: 4
Cooking Time: 20 Minutes

**Ingredients:**

- 1 green cabbage head, shredded
- Juice of ½ lemon
- A pinch of salt and black pepper
- ½ cup coconut cream
- ½ teaspoon fennel seeds
- 1 tablespoon mustard

**Directions:**

1. Combine all the ingredients in a suitable baking pan.
2. Cook in your air fryer at 350 degrees F/ 175 degrees C for 20 minutes.
3. Serve on plates as a side dish.

# Stuffed Peppers

Servings: 1
Cooking Time: 16 Minutes

**Ingredients:**

- 1 bell pepper
- ½ tablespoon diced onion
- ½ diced tomato, plus one tomato slice
- ¼ teaspoon smoked paprika
- Salt and pepper, to taste
- 1 teaspoon olive oil
- ¼ teaspoon dried basil

**Directions:**

1. Before cooking, heat your air fryer to 350 degrees F/ 175 degrees C.
2. The bell pepper should be cored and cleaned for stuffing.
3. Using half of the olive oil to brush the pepper on the outside.
4. Combine together the diced onion, the diced tomato, smoked paprika, salt, and pepper in a small bowl.
5. Then stuff the cored pepper with the mixture and add the tomato slice on the top.
6. Using the remaining olive oil, brush the tomato slice.
7. Sprinkle the stuffed pepper with basil.
8. Cook the stuffed peppers in your air fryer for 10 minutes or until thoroughly cooked.

# Mushroom Mozzarella Risotto

Servings: 4

Cooking Time: 20 Minutes

**Ingredients:**

- 1-pound white mushrooms, sliced
- ¼ cup mozzarella, shredded
- 1 cauliflower head, florets separated and riced
- 1 cup chicken stock
- 1 tablespoon thyme, chopped
- 1 teaspoon Italian seasoning
- A pinch of salt and black pepper
- 2 tablespoons olive oil

**Directions:**

1. Grease a suitable baking pan with oil and then heat to medium heat.
2. Add the cauliflower rice and mushrooms. Toss and cook for a few minutes.
3. Add the shredded mozzarella, chicken stock, Italian seasoning, salt, and black pepper in the pan.
4. Cook in your air fryer at 360 degrees F/ 180 degrees C for 20 minutes.
5. To serve, sprinkle the chopped thyme on the top.

# Maple Glazed Parsnips

Servings: 6

Cooking Time: 44 Minutes

**Ingredients:**

- 2 pounds parsnips, peeled
- 1 tablespoon butter, melted
- 2 tablespoons maple syrup
- 1 tablespoon dried parsley flakes, crushed
- ¼ teaspoon red pepper flakes, crushed

**Directions:**

1. Before cooking, heat your air fryer to 355 degrees F/ 180 degrees C.
2. Using cooking spray, spray the air fryer basket. Cut the peeled parsnips into 1-inch chunks.
3. In a bowl, add butter and parsnips and toss well to coat.
4. Then evenly arrange the parsnips on the air fryer basket.
5. Cook in your air fryer for about 40 minutes.
6. Then mix the remaining ingredients in a large bowl.
7. Transfer the mixture inside the air fryer basket.
8. Cook for about 4 minutes or more.
9. When cooked, remove from the air fryer and serve warm.

# Herbed Radishes

Servings:2
Cooking Time: 10 Minutes

**Ingredients:**

- 1 pound (454 g) radishes
- 2 tablespoons unsalted butter, melted
- ¼ teaspoon dried oregano
- ½ teaspoon dried parsley
- ½ teaspoon garlic powder

**Directions:**

1. Preheat the air fryer to 350ºF (177ºC). Prepare the radishes by cutting off their tops and bottoms and quartering them.
2. In a bowl, combine the butter, dried oregano, dried parsley, and garlic powder. Toss with the radishes to coat.
3. Transfer the radishes to the air fryer and air fry for 10 minutes, shaking the basket at the halfway point to ensure the radishes air fry evenly through. The radishes are ready when they turn brown.
4. Serve immediately.

# Broccoli Cheese Tots

Servings:4
Cooking Time: 15 Minutes

**Ingredients:**

- Olive oil
- 12 ounces frozen broccoli, thawed and drained
- 1 large egg
- 1½ teaspoons minced garlic
- ¼ cup grated Parmesan cheese
- ¼ cup shredded reduced-fat sharp Cheddar cheese
- ½ cup seasoned whole-wheat bread crumbs
- Salt
- Freshly ground black pepper

**Directions:**

1. Spray the fryer basket lightly with olive oil.
2. Gently squeeze the thawed broccoli to remove any excess liquid.
3. In a food processor, combine the broccoli, egg, garlic, Parmesan cheese, Cheddar cheese, bread crumbs, salt, and pepper and pulse until it resembles a coarse meal.
4. Using a tablespoon, scoop up the broccoli mixture and shape into 24 oval "tater tot" shapes.
5. Place the tots in the fryer basket in a single layer, being careful to space them a little bit apart. Lightly spray the tots with oil. You may need to cook them in batches.
6. Air fry for 6 to 7 minutes. Turn the tots over and cook for an additional 6 to 8 minutes or until lightly browned and crispy.

# Tasty Sweet Potato Wedges

Servings: 2
Cooking Time: 25 Minutes
**Ingredients:**

- 1 tablespoon olive oil
- ¼ teaspoon salt
- ½ teaspoon chili powder
- ½ teaspoon garlic powder
- ½ teaspoon smoked paprika
- ½ teaspoon dried thyme
- A pinch cayenne pepper

**Directions:**

1. In a suitable bowl, mix olive oil, salt, chili and garlic powder, smoked paprika, thyme, and cayenne.
2. Toss in the potato wedges. Arrange the wedges on the air fryer, and cook for 25 minutes at 380 degrees F/ 195 degrees C, flipping once.

# Tamari Green Beans

Servings: 2
Cooking Time: 10 Minutes
**Ingredients:**

- 8 ounces green beans, trimmed
- 1 teaspoon sesame oil
- 1 tablespoon tamari

**Directions:**

1. Add all the recipe ingredients into the suitable mixing bowl and toss well.
2. Grease its air fryer basket with cooking spray.
3. Transfer green beans in air fryer basket and cook at almost 400 degrees F/ 205 degrees C for almost 10 minutes. Toss halfway through.
4. Serve and enjoy.

# Vegetable Medley

Servings: 4
Cooking Time: 15 Minutes
**Ingredients:**

- 1 head broccoli, chopped (about 2 cups)
- 2 medium carrots, cut into 1-inch pieces
- Salt
- Pepper
- Cooking oil
- 1 zucchini, cut into 1-inch chunks
- 1 medium red bell pepper, seeded and thinly sliced

**Directions:**

1. In a large bowl, combine the broccoli and carrots. Season with salt and pepper to taste. Spray with cooking oil.
2. Transfer the broccoli and carrots to the air fryer basket. Cook for 6 minutes.
3. Place the zucchini and red pepper in the bowl. Season with salt and pepper to taste. Spray with cooking oil.
4. Add the zucchini and red pepper to the broccoli and carrots in the air fryer basket. Cook for 6 minutes.
5. Cool before serving.

# Garlicky Mushrooms With Parsley

Servings: 2
Cooking Time: 12 Minutes
**Ingredients:**

- 8 ounces mushrooms, sliced
- 1 tablespoon parsley, chopped
- 1 teaspoon soy sauce
- ½ teaspoon garlic powder
- 1 tablespoon olive oil
- Black pepper
- Salt

**Directions:**

1. Add all the recipe ingredients into the mixing bowl and toss well.
2. Transfer mushrooms in air fryer basket and cook at almost 380 degrees F/ 195 degrees C for almost 10-12 minutes. Shake basket halfway through.
3. Serve and enjoy.

# Zucchini Tots With Mozzarella

Servings: 4
Cooking Time: 6 Minutes
**Ingredients:**

- 1 zucchini, grated
- ½ cup Mozzarella, shredded
- 1 egg, beaten
- 2 tablespoons. almond flour
- ½ teaspoon black pepper
- 1 teaspoon coconut oil, melted

**Directions:**

1. Mix up grated zucchini, shredded Mozzarella, egg, almond flour, and black pepper.
2. Then make the small zucchini tots with the help of the fingertips.
3. At 385 degrees F/ 195 degrees C, preheat your air fryer.
4. Place the zucchini tots in the air fryer basket and cook for 3 minutes from each side or until the zucchini tots are golden brown.
5. Serve.

# Saltine Wax Beans

Servings:4
Cooking Time: 7 Minutes
**Ingredients:**

- ½ cup flour
- 1 teaspoon smoky chipotle powder
- ½ teaspoon ground black pepper
- 1 teaspoon sea salt flakes
- 2 eggs, beaten
- ½ cup crushed saltines
- 10 ounces (283 g) wax beans
- Cooking spray

**Directions:**

1. Preheat the air fryer to 360ºF (182ºC).
2. Combine the flour, chipotle powder, black pepper, and salt in a bowl. Put the eggs in a second bowl. Put the crushed saltines in a third bowl.
3. Wash the beans with cold water and discard any tough strings.
4. Coat the beans with the flour mixture, before dipping them into the beaten egg. Cover them with the crushed saltines.
5. Spritz the beans with cooking spray.
6. Air fry for 4 minutes. Give the air fryer basket a good shake and continue to air fry for 3 minutes. Serve hot.

# Parmesan Green Beans

Servings:4
Cooking Time: 7 Minutes
**Ingredients:**

- Olive oil
- 1 cup whole-wheat panko bread crumbs
- ¼ cup grated Parmesan cheese
- 1 teaspoon garlic powder
- ½ teaspoon freshly ground black pepper
- ½ teaspoon salt
- 1 egg
- 1 pound fresh green beans, trimmed

**Directions:**

1. Spray a fryer basket lightly with olive oil.
2. In a medium bowl, mix together the panko bread crumbs, Parmesan cheese, garlic powder, black pepper, and salt.
3. In a small, shallow bowl, whisk the egg.
4. Dip the green beans in the whisked egg and then coat in the panko bread crumb mixture.
5. Place the green beans in a single layer in the fryer basket. Spritz lightly with olive oil. You may need to cook more than one batch.
6. Air fry until light brown and crispy, 5 to 7 minutes.

# Zucchinis And Arugula Salad

Servings: 4
Cooking Time: 20 Minutes
**Ingredients:**

- 1-pound zucchinis, sliced
- 1 tablespoon olive oil
- Salt and white pepper to the taste
- 4 ounces arugula leaves
- ¼ cup chives, chopped
- 1 cup walnuts, chopped

**Directions:**

1. Combine the chopped chives, zucchini, olive oil, salt, and white pepper in the air fryer basket. Toss well.
2. Cook in your air fryer at 360 degrees F/ 180 degrees C for 20 minutes.
3. Place the cooked veggies in a salad bowl and toss with the walnuts and arugula.
4. Serve as a side salad.

# Roasted Brown Butter Carrots

Servings: 4
Cooking Time: 20 Minutes
**Ingredients:**

- 1 tablespoon unsalted butter
- 6 carrots, cut into ½-inch pieces (about 3 cups)
- Salt
- Pepper

**Directions:**

1. Place a saucepan over high heat. Add the butter. Allow the butter to melt for 2 to 3 minutes.
2. Stirring constantly to ensure it does not scorch, cook for 1 to 2 minutes, until it starts to turn brown. Brown bits will form on the bottom of the pan. Remove the pan from heat.
3. In a large bowl, combine the carrots with the brown butter. Season with salt and pepper to taste.
4. Transfer the carrots to the air fryer. Cook for 6 minutes.
5. Open the air fryer and shake the basket. Cook for an additional 6 minutes.
6. Cool before serving.

# Mushroom And Pepper Pizza Squares

Servings:10
Cooking Time: 10 Minutes
**Ingredients:**

- 1 pizza dough, cut into squares
- 1 cup chopped oyster mushrooms
- 1 shallot, chopped
- ¼ red bell pepper, chopped
- 2 tablespoons parsley
- Salt and ground black pepper, to taste

**Directions:**

1. Preheat the air fryer to 400ºF (204ºC).
2. In a bowl, combine the oyster mushrooms, shallot, bell pepper and parsley. Sprinkle some salt and pepper as desired.
3. Spread this mixture on top of the pizza squares.
4. Bake in the air fryer for 10 minutes.
5. Serve warm.

# Creamy Cauliflower Puree

Servings: 2
Cooking Time: 8 Minutes

**Ingredients:**

- 1 ½ cup cauliflower, chopped
- 1 tablespoon butter, melted
- ½ teaspoon salt
- 1 tablespoon fresh parsley, chopped
- ¼ cup heavy cream
- Cooking spray

**Directions:**

1. Spritz the cooking spray over the inside of the air fryer basket.
2. Place the chopped cauliflower in the air fryer basket.
3. Cook in your air fryer at 400 degrees F/ 205 degrees C for 8 minutes. Stir the cauliflower every 4 minutes.
4. Heat the heavy cream until it is hot. Then pour in a blender, add parsley, butter, salt, and cauliflower.
5. Blend until it is smooth.

# Balsamic Brussels Sprouts

Servings: 6
Cooking Time: 10 Minutes

**Ingredients:**

- 2 cups Brussels sprouts, sliced
- 1 tablespoon balsamic vinegar
- 1 tablespoon olive oil
- ¼ teaspoon salt

**Directions:**

1. Add all the recipe ingredients into the suitable bowl and toss well.
2. Grease its air fryer basket with cooking spray.
3. Transfer Brussels sprouts mixture into the air fryer basket.
4. Cook Brussels sprouts at 400 degrees F/ 205 degrees C for almost 10 minutes. Shake basket halfway through.
5. Serve and enjoy.

# Creamy And Cheesy Spinach

Servings:4
Cooking Time: 15 Minutes
**Ingredients:**

- Vegetable oil spray
- 1 (10-ounce / 283-g) package frozen spinach, thawed and squeezed dry
- ½ cup chopped onion
- 2 cloves garlic, minced
- 4 ounces (113 g) cream cheese, diced
- ½ teaspoon ground nutmeg
- 1 teaspoon kosher salt
- 1 teaspoon black pepper
- ½ cup grated Parmesan cheese

**Directions:**

1. Preheat the air fryer to 350ºF (177ºC). Spray a heatproof pan with vegetable oil spray.
2. In a medium bowl, combine the spinach, onion, garlic, cream cheese, nutmeg, salt, and pepper. Transfer to the prepared pan.
3. Put the pan in the air fryer basket. Bake for 10 minutes. Open and stir to thoroughly combine the cream cheese and spinach.
4. Sprinkle the Parmesan cheese on top. Bake for 5 minutes, or until the cheese has melted and browned.
5. Serve hot.

# Desserts And Sweets
## Simple Donuts

Servings: 4
Cooking Time: 15 Minutes
**Ingredients:**

- 8 ounces' coconut flour 2 tablespoons stevia
- 1 egg, whisked
- 1-½ tablespoons butter, melted
- 4 ounces' coconut milk
- 1 teaspoon baking powder

**Directions:**

1. Thoroughly mix up all of the ingredients in a bowl.
2. Form donuts from the mixture.
3. Cook the donuts in your air fryer at 370 degrees F/ 185 degrees C for 15 minutes.
4. When cooked, serve and enjoy.

# Chocolate Banana Brownie

Servings: 4
Cooking Time: 16 Minutes
**Ingredients:**
- 1 cup bananas, overripe
- 1 scoop protein: powder
- 2 tablespoons unsweetened cocoa powder
- ½ cup almond butter, melted

**Directions:**
1. Before cooking, heat your air fryer to 325 degrees F/ 160 degrees C.
2. Using cooking spray, spray a baking pan that fits in your air fryer.
3. In a blender, mix the bananas, protein powder, cocoa powder, and the almond butter together until smooth.
4. Spread the better onto the baking pan.
5. Cook the brownie in the preheated air fryer for 16 minutes.
6. Serve and enjoy!

# Pineapple And Chocolate Cake

Servings:4
Cooking Time: 35 To 40 Minutes
**Ingredients:**
- 2 cups flour
- 4 ounces (113 g) butter, melted
- ¼ cup sugar
- ½ pound (227 g) pineapple, chopped
- ½ cup pineapple juice
- 1 ounce (28 g) dark chocolate, grated
- 1 large egg
- 2 tablespoons skimmed milk

**Directions:**
1. Preheat the air fryer to 370ºF (188ºC).
2. Grease a cake tin with a little oil or butter.
3. In a bowl, combine the butter and flour to create a crumbly consistency.
4. Add the sugar, chopped pineapple, juice, and grated dark chocolate and mix well.
5. In a separate bowl, combine the egg and milk. Add this mixture to the flour mixture and stir well until a soft dough forms.
6. Pour the mixture into the cake tin and transfer to the air fryer.
7. Bake for 35 to 40 minutes.
8. Serve immediately.

# Oatmeal Raisin Bars

Servings:8
Cooking Time: 15 Minutes
**Ingredients:**

- ⅓ cup all-purpose flour
- ¼ teaspoon kosher salt
- ¼ teaspoon baking powder
- ¼ teaspoon ground cinnamon
- ¼ cup light brown sugar, lightly packed
- ¼ cup granulated sugar

- ½ cup canola oil
- 1 large egg
- 1 teaspoon vanilla extract
- 1⅓ cups quick-cooking oats
- ⅓ cup raisins

**Directions:**

1. Preheat the air fryer to 360ºF (182ºC).
2. In a large bowl, combine the all-purpose flour, kosher salt, baking powder, ground cinnamon, light brown sugar, granulated sugar, canola oil, egg, vanilla extract, quick-cooking oats, and raisins.
3. Spray a baking pan with nonstick cooking spray, then pour the oat mixture into the pan and press down to evenly distribute. Place the pan in the air fryer and bake for 15 minutes or until golden brown.
4. Remove from the air fryer and allow to cool in the pan on a wire rack for 20 minutes before slicing and serving.

# Lemon Creamy Muffins

Servings: 6
Cooking Time: 11 Minutes
**Ingredients:**

- 1 cup almond flour
- 3 tablespoons Erythritol
- 1 scoop protein: powder
- 1 teaspoon vanilla extract
- 3 tablespoons coconut oil, melted
- 1 egg, beaten
- ½ teaspoon baking powder
- ½ teaspoon instant coffee
- 1 teaspoon lemon juice
- 2 tablespoons heavy cream
- Cooking spray

**Directions:**

1. After adding the almond flour, Erythritol, protein: powder, vanilla extract, coconut oil, egg, baking powder, instant coffee, lemon juice, and heavy cream in a suitable bowl, use the immersion blender to whisk them until smooth.
2. Spray the muffin molds with cooking spray.
3. Fill half of each muffin mold with muffin batter and arrange them to the cooking basket of your air fryer.
4. Cook them at 360 degrees F/ 180 degrees C for 11 minutes.
5. When done, serve and enjoy.

# Jelly Doughnuts

Servings:8
Cooking Time: 5 Minutes
**Ingredients:**

- 1 (16.3-ounce / 462-g) package large refrigerator biscuits
- Cooking spray
- 1¼ cups good-quality raspberry jam
- Confectioners' sugar, for dusting

**Directions:**

1. Preheat the air fryer to 350°F (177°C).
2. Separate biscuits into 8 rounds. Spray both sides of rounds lightly with oil.
3. Spray the basket with oil and place 3 to 4 rounds in the basket. Air fry for 5 minutes, or until golden brown. Transfer to a wire rack; let cool. Repeat with the remaining rounds.
4. Fill a pastry bag, fitted with small plain tip, with raspberry jam; use tip to poke a small hole in the side of each doughnut, then fill the centers with the jam. Dust doughnuts with confectioners' sugar.
5. Serve immediately.

# Oatmeal And Carrot Cookie Cups

Servings:16
Cooking Time: 8 Minutes
**Ingredients:**

- 3 tablespoons unsalted butter, at room temperature
- ¼ cup packed brown sugar
- 1 tablespoon honey
- 1 egg white
- ½ teaspoon vanilla extract
- ⅓ cup finely grated carrot
- ½ cup quick-cooking oatmeal
- ⅓ cup whole-wheat pastry flour
- ½ teaspoon baking soda
- ¼ cup dried cherries

**Directions:**

1. Preheat the air fryer to 350°F (177°C)
2. In a medium bowl, beat the butter, brown sugar, and honey until well combined.
3. Add the egg white, vanilla, and carrot. Beat to combine.
4. Stir in the oatmeal, pastry flour, and baking soda.
5. Stir in the dried cherries.
6. Double up 32 mini muffin foil cups to make 16 cups. Fill each with about 4 teaspoons of dough. Bake the cookie cups, 8 at a time, for 8 minutes, or until light golden brown and just set. Serve warm.

# Black Forest Pies

Servings: 6
Cooking Time: 15 Minutes
**Ingredients:**

- 3 tablespoons milk or dark chocolate chips
- 2 tablespoons thick, hot fudge sauce
- 2 tablespoons chopped dried cherries
- 1 (10-by-15-inch) sheet frozen puff pastry, thawed
- 1 egg white, beaten
- 2 tablespoons sugar
- ½ teaspoon cinnamon

**Directions:**

1. Preheat the air fryer to 350ºF (177ºC).
2. In a small bowl, combine the chocolate chips, fudge sauce, and dried cherries.
3. Roll out the puff pastry on a floured surface. Cut into 6 squares with a sharp knife.
4. Divide the chocolate chip mixture into the center of each puff pastry square. Fold the squares in half to make triangles. Firmly press the edges with the tines of a fork to seal.
5. Brush the triangles on all sides sparingly with the beaten egg white. Sprinkle the tops with sugar and cinnamon.
6. Put in the air fryer basket and bake for 15 minutes or until the triangles are golden brown. The filling will be hot, so cool for at least 20 minutes before serving.

# Vanilla Banana Puffs

Servings: 8
Cooking Time: 10 Min.
**Ingredients:**

- 4 ounces instant vanilla pudding
- 4 ounces cream cheese, softened
- 1 package (8-ounce) crescent dinner rolls, refrigerated
- 1 cup milk
- 2 bananas, sliced
- 1 egg, lightly beaten

**Directions:**

1. On a flat kitchen surface, plug your air fryer and turn it on.
2. Before cooking, heat your air fryer to 355 degrees F/ 180 degrees C for about 4 to 5 minutes.
3. Make 8 squares from the crescent dinner rolls.
4. Mix thoroughly the milk and pudding in a medium sized bowl. Then whisk the cream cheese in the mixture.
5. Divide the mixture onto the squares. Add the banana slices on the top.
6. Fold the rolls over and press the edges to seal the filling inside. Brush the whisked egg over each pastry puff.
7. Transfer to the air fryer basket.
8. Cook the banana puffs in the preheated air fryer for 10 minutes.
9. When the cooking time runs out, remove from the air fryer and serve warm.
10. Enjoy!

# Vanilla Cobbler With Hazelnut

Servings: 4
Cooking Time: 30 Minutes
**Ingredients:**

- ¼ cup heavy cream
- 1 egg, beaten
- ½ cup almond flour
- 1 teaspoon vanilla extract
- 2 tablespoons butter, softened
- ¼ cup hazelnuts, chopped

**Directions:**

1. Mix up heavy cream, egg, almond flour, vanilla extract, and butter.
2. Then whisk the mixture gently. At 325 degrees F/ 160 degrees C, preheat your air fryer.
3. Layer its air fryer basket with baking paper.
4. Pour ½ part of the batter in the baking pan, flatten it gently and top with hazelnuts.
5. Then pour the remaining batter over the hazelnuts and place the pan in the air fryer.
6. Cook the cobbler for 30 minutes.

# Chocolate Peanut Butter Bread Pudding

Servings:8
Cooking Time: 10 To 12 Minutes
**Ingredients:**

- Nonstick baking spray with flour
- 1 egg
- 1 egg yolk
- ¾ cup chocolate milk
- 2 tablespoons cocoa powder
- 3 tablespoons brown sugar
- 3 tablespoons peanut butter
- 1 teaspoon vanilla
- 5 slices firm white bread, cubed

**Directions:**

1. Spray a 6-by-6-by-2-inch baking pan with nonstick spray.
2. In a medium bowl, combine the egg, egg yolk, chocolate milk, cocoa, brown sugar, peanut butter, and vanilla, and mix until combined. Stir in the bread cubes and let soak for 10 minutes.
3. Spoon this mixture into the prepared pan. Bake for 10 to 12 minutes or until the pudding is firm to the touch.

# Enticing Chocolate Cake

Servings: 6
Cooking Time: 30 Minutes

**Ingredients:**

- 2 eggs, beaten
- ⅔ cup sour cream
- 1 cup almond flour
- ⅔ cup swerve
- ⅓ cup coconut oil, softened
- ¼ cup cocoa powder
- 2 tablespoons chocolate chips, unsweetened
- 1 ½ teaspoons baking powder
- 1 teaspoon vanilla extract
- ½ teaspoon pure rum extract
- Chocolate Frosting:
- ½ cup butter, softened
- ¼ cup cocoa powder
- 1 cup powdered swerve
- 2 tablespoons milk

**Directions:**

1. Mix all the recipe ingredients for the chocolate cake with a hand mixer on low speed.
2. Scrape the batter into a cake pan.
3. Air fry at 330 degrees F/ 165 degrees C for 25 to 30 minutes.
4. Then transfer the cake to a wire rack to cool.
5. Meanwhile, whip the butter and cocoa until smooth.
6. Add the powdered swerve. Slowly and gradually, pour in the milk until your frosting reaches desired consistency.
7. Whip until smooth and fluffy; then, frost the cooled cake.
8. Place the frosted cake in your refrigerator for a couple of hours.
9. Serve well chilled.

# Chickpea Brownies

Servings:6

Cooking Time: 20 Minutes

**Ingredients:**

- Vegetable oil
- 1 (15-ounce / 425-g) can chickpeas, drained and rinsed
- 4 large eggs
- ⅓ cup coconut oil, melted
- ⅓ cup honey
- 3 tablespoons unsweetened cocoa powder
- 1 tablespoon espresso powder (optional)
- 1 teaspoon baking powder
- 1 teaspoon baking soda
- ½ cup chocolate chips

**Directions:**

1. Preheat the air fryer to 325°F (163°C).
2. Generously grease a baking pan with vegetable oil.
3. In a blender or food processor, combine the chickpeas, eggs, coconut oil, honey, cocoa powder, espresso powder (if using), baking powder, and baking soda. Blend or process until smooth. Transfer to the prepared pan and stir in the chocolate chips by hand.
4. Set the pan in the air fryer basket and bake for 20 minutes, or until a toothpick inserted into the center comes out clean.
5. Let cool in the pan on a wire rack for 30 minutes before cutting into squares.
6. Serve immediately.

# Banana Slices With Cardamom

Servings: 8
Cooking Time: 15 Minutes

**Ingredients:**

- 4 medium ripe bananas, peeled
- ⅓ cup rice flour, divided
- 2 tablespoons all-purpose flour
- 2 tablespoons corn flour
- 2 tablespoons desiccated coconut
- ½ teaspoon baking powder
- ½ teaspoon ground cardamom
- Pinch of salt
- Water, as required
- ¼ cup sesame seeds

**Directions:**

1. In a suitable bowl, mix 2 tablespoons of rice flour, all-purpose flour, cornmeal, coconut, baking powder, cardamom and salt.
2. Add the water in the bowl and mix until a thick, smooth dough forms.
3. In another bowl, place the remaining rice flour.
4. In a third bowl, add the sesame seeds.
5. Cut each banana in ½ and then cut each ½ into 2 pieces lengthwise.
6. Dip the banana into the coconut mixture and then top with the remaining rice flour, followed by the sesame seeds.
7. Select the "Air Fry" mode and set the cooking time to 15 minutes.
8. Set the temperature setting to 390 degrees F/ 200 degrees C.
9. Arrange banana slices in air fry basket and place in air fryer.
10. Transfer banana slices to plates to cool slightly.

# Zucchini Bars With Cream Cheese

Servings: 12
Cooking Time: 15 Minutes
**Ingredients:**

- 3 tablespoons coconut oil, melted 6 eggs
- 3 ounces' zucchini, shredded 2 teaspoons vanilla extract
- ½ teaspoon baking powder
- 4 ounces' cream cheese
- 2 tablespoons erythritol

**Directions:**

1. Whisk the coconut oil, zucchini, vanilla extract, baking powder, cream cheese, and erythritol in a bowl, then pour in the cooking pan lined with parchment paper.
2. Cook at 320 degrees F/ 160 degrees C for 15 minutes.
3. Slice and cool down.
4. Serve and enjoy.

# Cinnamon Crunch S'mores

Servings:12
Cooking Time: 10 Minutes
**Ingredients:**

- 12 whole cinnamon graham crackers
- 2 (1.55-ounce) chocolate bars, broken into 12 pieces
- 12 marshmallows

**Directions:**

1. Halve each graham cracker into 2 squares.
2. Place 6 graham cracker squares in the air fryer. Do not stack. Place a piece of chocolate onto each. Cook for 2 minutes.
3. Open the air fryer and add a marshmallow onto each piece of melted chocolate. Cook for 1 additional minute.
4. Remove the cooked s'mores from the air fryer, then repeat steps 2 and 3 for the remaining 6 s'mores.
5. Top with the remaining graham cracker squares and serve.

# Sweet Blackberry Cream

Servings: 6
Cooking Time: 20 Minutes
**Ingredients:**

- 2 cups blackberries
- Juice of ½ lemon
- 2 tablespoons water
- 1 teaspoon vanilla extract
- 2 tablespoons swerve

**Directions:**

1. In a suitable bowl, mix all the recipe ingredients and whisk well.
2. Divide this into 6 ramekins, put them in a preheated air fryer and cook at almost 340 degrees F/ 170 degrees C for 20 minutes.
3. Cool down and serve.

# Erythritol Pineapple Slices

Servings: 4
Cooking Time: 20 Minutes
**Ingredients:**

- 4 pineapple slices
- 1 teaspoon cinnamon
- 2 tablespoons Erythritol

**Directions:**

1. Add pineapple slices, sweetener, and cinnamon into the zip-lock bag.
2. Shake well and keep in the refrigerator for 30 minutes.
3. At 350 degrees F/ 175 degrees C, preheat your air fryer.
4. Place pineapples slices into the air fryer basket and cook for 20 minutes.
5. Turn halfway through.
6. Serve and enjoy.

# Donuts

Servings: 14 Donuts
Cooking Time: 2 Hours

**Ingredients:**

- 3 cups of all-purpose flour
- 1 cup of milk, warmed to around 110°F
- 4 tablespoons of unsalted melted butter
- 1 large egg
- ¼ cup +1 teaspoon of sugar
- 2 ½ teaspoons of active dry yeast
- ½ teaspoon of kosher salt
- For Glaze:
- 2 cups of powdered sugar
- 6 tablespoons of unsalted melted butter
- 2 teaspoons of vanilla extract
- 2–4 tablespoons of hot water

**Directions:**

1. Add the warm milk, yeast, and 1 teaspoon of sugar to a large bowl. Stir it for 5–10 minutes until foamy.

2. Add the egg, ¼ cup of sugar, and salt into the milk mixture. Stir it until combined. Pour in the melted butter with 2 cups of flour and mix.

3. Scrape the sides of the bowl down, and add in 1 more cup of flour. Mix it well until the dough starts pulling away from the bowl but leaves sticky. Continue kneading for 5–10 minutes. Cover the bowl with plastic wrap. Leave it for 30 minutes until the dough doubled.

4. Spread some flour on the work surface. Transfer the dough onto it and roll into a ½-¼-inch-thick layer. Cut out donuts with a round cutter (about 3 inches in diameter). Use a smaller cutter (about 1 inch in diameter) and cut out the centers.

5. Transfer the formed donuts onto the oiled parchment paper, and cover them with oiled plastic wrap. Leave it for 20–30 minutes until the dough is doubled.

6. Preheat your air fryer to 350°F. Spray the inside of the basket with some oil.

7. Put the formed donuts in the preheated air fryer in a single layer. Avoid them touching. Lightly spray tops with oil. Cook at 350°F for 4–5 minutes. Repeat this step with the remaining part of donuts and their holes.

8. For making glaze: Meantime, pour the melted butter into a medium bowl. Add in vanilla and powdered sugar. Whisk until combined. Stir in 1 tablespoon of hot water at a time until you reach the desired consistency.

9. After cooling the cooked donuts for a few minutes, glaze them until fully coated. Put donuts on the rack to drip off the excess of the glaze until it hardens.

10. Serve and enjoy your Donuts!

# Bourbon Bread Pudding

Servings:4
Cooking Time: 20 Minutes
**Ingredients:**

- 3 slices whole grain bread, cubed
- 1 large egg
- 1 cup whole milk
- 2 tablespoons bourbon
- ½ teaspoons vanilla extract
- ¼ cup maple syrup, divided
- ½ teaspoons ground cinnamon
- 2 teaspoons sparkling sugar

**Directions:**

1. Preheat the air fryer to 270ºF (132ºC).
2. Spray a baking pan with nonstick cooking spray, then place the bread cubes in the pan.
3. In a medium bowl, whisk together the egg, milk, bourbon, vanilla extract, 3 tablespoons of maple syrup, and cinnamon. Pour the egg mixture over the bread and press down with a spatula to coat all the bread, then sprinkle the sparkling sugar on top and bake for 20 minutes.
4. Remove the pudding from the air fryer and allow to cool in the pan on a wire rack for 10 minutes. Drizzle the remaining 1 tablespoon of maple syrup on top. Slice and serve warm.

# Cookies With Mashed Strawberry

Servings: 4
Cooking Time: 9 Minutes
**Ingredients:**

- 2 teaspoons butter, softened
- 1 tablespoon Splenda
- 1 egg yolk
- ½ cup almond flour
- 1 oz. strawberry, chopped, mashed

**Directions:**

1. In a suitable bowl, mix the butter, Splenda, egg yolk and almond flour well. Knead the non-sticky dough.
2. Form the small balls from the dough and use your finger to make small holes in each ball.
3. Fill the balls with the mashed strawberries.
4. Arrange to the balls to the cooking pan lined with baking paper and cook them at 360 degrees F/ 180 degrees C for 9 minutes.
5. When done, serve and enjoy.

# Recipe Index

Grilled Butter Sandwich 13

Grilled Cheese Sandwich 20

Grilled Curried Chicken Wings 34

Grouper With Miso-honey Sauce 61

Garlic Chicken With Bacon 38

Garlic Cauliflower Appetizer 30

Garlic Pork Roast 48

Garlicky Mushrooms With Parsley 73

Ginger-garlic Swordfish 67

**H**

Herbed Radishes 71

Herbs Chicken Drumsticks With Tamari Sauce 45

Healthy Chicken With Veggies 35

Healthy Salmon With Cardamom 60

Haddock Cakes 61

Hard-boiled Eggs 17

**J**

Jelly Doughnuts 81

**K**

Korean Short Ribs 54

**L**

Lemon Breaded Fish 63

Lemon Creamy Muffins 80

Lemony Cabbage Slaw 69

Lemony Endive In Curried Yogurt 27

Lamb Meatballs 46

**M**

Mexican Beef Muffins With Tomato Sauce 30

Mushroom Mozzarella Risotto 70

Roasted Almonds With Paprika 25

Rosemary Chicken With Lemon Wedges 44

## S

Seasoned Turkey Meat With Kale 36

Squash Chips With Sauce 23

Steak Mushroom Bites 55

Steak With Onion And Bell Peppers 47

Strawberry And Peach Toast 22

Stuffed Bell Peppers With Mayonnaise 68

Stuffed Peppers 69

Sumptuous Pizza Tortilla Rolls 56

Sweet Blackberry Cream 88

Sweet Marinated Chicken Wings 42

Sweet And Sour Glazed Salmon 62

Salmon Burgers 58

Saltine Wax Beans 74

Sausage And Egg Breakfast Burrito 15

Simple Cherry Tarts 16

Simple Donuts 78

Simple Scotch Eggs 21

Southwest Stuffed Mushrooms 28

Southwestern Prawns With Asparagus 57

Spanish Garlic Shrimp 58

Spice Chicken With Broccoli 43

Spice Meatloaf 45

Spiced Beef Chuck Roast 55

Spicy Chicken Stir-fry 39

Spicy And Crispy Duck 36

Spicy Orange Shrimp 65

Printed in Great Britain
by Amazon

37702794R00057